FUNDAMENTALS
OF WRITING
FOR A
SPECIFIC PURPOSE

PRENTICE-HALL, INC., Englewood Cliffs, New Jersey 07632

Sandra McKay
San Francisco State University

FUNDAMENTALS OF WRITING FOR A SPECIFIC PURPOSE

Library of Congress Cataloging in Publication Data

MCKAY, SANDRA.
  Fundamentals of writing for a specific purpose.

  Includes index.
    1. English language—Text-books for foreigners.
2. English language—Rhetoric. 3. English
language—Grammar—1950–   I. Title.
PE1128.M368   808′.042   82-5328
ISBN 0-13-344895-9   AACR2

Editorial production, supervision,
  and interior design by F. Hubert
Cover design by Debbie Watson from a
  concept by Prudence Kohler
Manufacturing buyer: Harry P. Baisley

Printed in the United States of America
10 9 8 7 6 5 4 3 2

ISBN 0-13-344895-9

PRENTICE-HALL INTERNATIONAL, INC., *London*
PRENTICE-HALL OF AUSTRALIA PTY. LIMITED, *Sydney*
PRENTICE-HALL CANADA INC., *Toronto*
PRENTICE-HALL OF INDIA PRIVATE LIMITED, *New Delhi*
PRENTICE-HALL OF JAPAN, INC., *Tokyo*
PRENTICE-HALL OF SOUTHEAST ASIA PTE. LTD., *Singapore*
WHITEHALL BOOKS LIMITED, *Wellington, New Zealand*

To Jerry and Michael

Contents

Preface   xiii

    Acknowledgments   xv

I
DESCRIBING   1

1
Describing a Process   3

    Grammatical Focus
    imperatives   4
    imperatives, third person singular -s, articles   5

    Rhetorical Focus
    sentence connectors of chronological order   7
    placement of adverbs   8

    Reading Selection   9

    Writing Tasks   11

    Peer Correction of Student Compositions   16

2
Describing an Object   17

Grammatical Focus
the verb to be, *subject–verb agreement*   18

Mechanical Focus
capitals, periods, commas with a series of items   20

Rhetorical Focus
descriptive nouns and adjectives of shape   22

Reading Selection   26

Writing Tasks   28

Peer Correction of Student Compositions   31

3
Describing a Place   33

Grammatical Focus
subject–verb agreement   34
articles   35
prepositions with expressions of place   37

Rhetorical Focus
descriptive adjectives   41

Reading Selection   42

Writing Tasks   43

Peer Correction of Student Compositions   47

4
Describing a Personality   51

Grammatical Focus
past tense   52
pronoun reference   52
expressions of quantity with count and noncount nouns   53
nonrestrictive relative clauses   54

Mechanical Focus
commas with nonrestrictive relative clauses   54

Rhetorical Focus
descriptive adjectives of human characteristics 56
relevancy of support 57

Reading Selection 59

Writing Tasks 61

Peer Correction of Student Compositions 63

5
Describing an Event 65

Grammatical Focus
verb tense: past progressive, past perfect 66
adverbial clauses of time 68
participial phrases 69

Mechanical Focus
commas with adverbial clauses of time 68
commas with participial phrases 69

Rhetorical Focus
action verbs 70
point of view 72

Reading Selection 73

Writing Tasks 75

Peer Correction of Student Compositions 78

II
DEFINING 81

6
Defining by Example 83

Grammatical Focus
passive voice 84
appositives 86

Mechanical Focus
commas with appositives 86

Rhetorical Focus
parallel structure with infinitives and gerunds 88
sentence connectors of exemplification 88

Reading Selection 90

Writing Tasks 92

Peer Correction of Student Compositions 96

7
Defining by Classification 97

Grammatical Focus
verb tense: present perfect 98
review of nonrestrictive relative clauses 99
review of the passive voice 101

Mechanical Focus
colons introducing categories 99

Rhetorical Focus
sentence connectors of classification 102
dividing a topic 104
categorizing data 105
conciseness 108

Reading Selection 109

Writing Tasks 110

Peer Correction of Student Compositions 116

8
Defining by Comparison and Contrast 117

Grammatical Focus
cohesive devices to replace nouns 118

Mechanical Focus
commas and semicolons with transitional phrases 122
semicolons joining sentences 126

Rhetorical Focus
sentence connectors of comparison and contrast   122
analogies   124
parallel sentence structure   126

Reading Selection   128

Writing Tasks   130

Peer Correction of Student Compositions   135

III
EXPRESSING AN OPINION   137

9
Expressing and Supporting an Opinion   139

Grammatical Focus
demonstratives as cohesive devices   140
subordinate clauses   142
direct and indirect speech   143

Mechanical Focus
punctuation of subordinate clauses   142
punctuation of quotations   143

Rhetorical Focus
expressions of opinion   144
statements of reason   147

Reading Selection   148

Writing Tasks   149

Peer Correction of Student Compositions   153

10
Ranking   155

Grammatical Focus
the expletive there   156
cleft sentences   159
parallel structure: not only . . . but also   161

Rhetorical Focus
expressing priorities   162

Reading Selection   165

Writing Tasks   166

Peer Correction of Student Compositions   170

11
Speculating   173

Grammatical Focus
conditional sentences   174

Mechanical Focus
commas with conditional sentences   174
commas and semicolons with transitional phrases   178

Rhetorical Focus
expressing hypothetical situations   177
expressions of cause and effect   178

Reading Selection   181

Writing Tasks   182

Peer Correction of Student Compositions   185

Index   187

Preface

Composing involves the dual task of deciding what to say and how to say it. Perhaps because of the concern with grammatical accuracy in ESL classes, the emphasis in teaching composition has frequently been on how to say it. Many lower and intermediate level ESL composition texts appear to equate the manipulating of sentence structure with the act of composing. By doing so, they focus on the end product rather than the *process* of composition—a process that involves such things as the selection of topic, organization pattern, and voice.

The basic assumption of this text is that a good writing text gives attention to the classical concerns of invention (the selection of topic), as well as to arrangement (effective organization), and style (acceptable grammar and diction). Furthermore, the text is based on the conviction that what goes on in a composition class should be relevant both to students' immediate academic needs and to their future career goals. In short, this text attempts to integrate the rhetorical and grammatical aspects of writing and to relate these two areas to a wide range of academic fields. It is intended for intermediate students who are pursuing an academic or professional degree.

As in the author's *Writing for a Specific Purpose*, students are provided with a situation and specific writing tasks from a wide range of professional fields. Thus the text is applicable to composition classes in which students have very different academic goals. The text begins with simple description, then moves to defining, and ends with expressing opinions. The text gives explicit attention to prevalent grammatical problems, but the grammar is always related to the rhetorical pattern. For example, describing a process will naturally draw on the use of imperatives (e.g., *Follow* these simple steps). Thus, in the chapter on describing a process, attention is given to this particular grammatical structure.

In this way, the materials support the idea that a good composition text must integrate the rhetorical and grammatical aspect of writing.

The text focuses on three main rhetorical strategies: *describing, defining,* and *expressing an opinion.* The first two are included because they occur in the writing of all academic fields. (An engineer, just like a business executive, is often called on to describe a process or define a concept.) The last area, expressing an opinion, provides an introduction to more complex forms of expository writing such as argumentation and persuasion. These three overall strategies are further broken down to topics such as describing a process, describing an object, and describing a place.

Each chapter begins with several controlled exercises dealing with the particular grammatical and rhetorical points that will be used in the writing tasks. For example, describing an object often makes use of the verb *to be* and descriptive adjectives of shape (e.g., A compass *is* a *circular* instrument for telling directions). Thus, the grammar focus of the chapter is the verb *to be* and the rhetorical focus is descriptive adjectives of shape. (The rhetorical exercises involve organizational strategies, as well as the selection of appropriate sentence connectors and lexical items.) Some chapters also include pertinent exercises on punctuation. Since classification often entails the use of colons (e.g., There are three major groups:), the chapter on classification contains an exercise on this point.

A brief reading selection that exemplifies the rhetorical pattern of the chapter is then presented, in order to reinforce the grammatical and rhetorical focus of the chapter and to illustrate typical methods of organization. For example, the chapter on describing a place has a reading selection that describes a typical Swahili home. The selection exemplifies the use of articles and prepositions, the grammatical focus of the chapter. Furthermore, the passage illustrates a typical rhetorical strategy of this type of essay, namely, to describe a place as if entering it from the outside. Each reading passage is followed by a series of questions which are designed to help students notice the relevant grammatical and rhetorical patterns.

Each chapter then presents a variety of writing situations and tasks. The first situations in each chapter are highly controlled, followed by less guided tasks. Furthermore, the first part of the text is limited to essays of one paragraph. Slightly longer essays are required in Part III. Thus, the text develops from simpler to more complex grammatical and rhetorical topics and proceeds from one-paragraph writing to longer essays. In order to provide the students with highly concrete and immediate writing tasks, visuals and specific problem-solving strategies are used.

Finally, each chapter concludes with some type of peer correction exercise. To further reinforce the grammatical and rhetorical focus of the chapter, the required corrections emphasize the concerns of the initial controlled exercises. However, very prevalent problems such as the use of articles and prepositions are included in many of the correction exercises. In addition, for review purposes, grammar topics that have been dealt with in earlier chapters appear again in later exercises.

Acknowledgments

I wish to thank the following people for their help in completing this text. Special thanks are due to Tony Bernakis, Margaret Grant, and Dorothy Petitt for their constructive suggestions, and to Claudia Wilson for her careful typing of the final manuscript. Thanks are also due to my students for their honest reactions to the materials as they were being developed. Finally, and most important, I wish to thank my husband for his help in typing and editing the manuscript and to my family for their support.

FUNDAMENTALS OF WRITING FOR A SPECIFIC PURPOSE

I

DESCRIBING

1. Describing a Process
2. Describing an Object
3. Describing a Place
4. Describing a Personality
5. Describing an Event

1

Describing a Process

Sometimes when you describe a process, all that is necessary is to explain how something is done. In these cases, the steps for completing the process are merely listed and the verb is in the imperative form (e.g., *Press* the valve). At other times describing a process includes not only how something is done, but why it is done and what is needed to complete the process.

EXERCISE 1.1

grammatical focus: imperatives

The following passage describes how to operate a fire extinguisher. Numbering the steps allows the reader to quickly follow the correct procedure.
Underline all the verbs in the imperative form in these directions.

1. Remove extinguisher from wall and shake can well.
2. Hold upright.
3. Direct nozzle at base of flame.
4. To discharge, press black valve all the way down.

The following passage describes how to make a periscope. Notice that in this case the directions are given in paragraph form.
Underline all the verbs in the imperative form in the following paragraph.

Periscopes are used in submarines and space capsules to see around a corner. A simple periscope requires only a mirror, a stick about two feet long, and a small block of wood. Cut the block of wood so that each edge is as long as the mirror. Next, cut the block in half diagonally. Attach half the block to the end of the stick and glue the mirror on the diagonal cut. You can now hold the stick and project the mirror section to see around a corner.

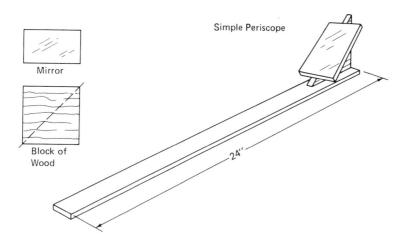

Simple Periscope

Mirror

Block of
Wood

24"

EXERCISE 1.2

grammatical focus: imperatives, third person singular -s, articles

The use of the imperative is very common in cookbooks. The following paragraph describes how to make muffins. Underline all the verbs in the imperative form in the recipe.

1 3/4 cups sifted flour	1 egg, beaten well
2 tsp. baking powder	3/4 cup milk
2 tbsp. sugar	1/3 cup shortening or salad oil
3/4 tsp. salt	

Sift dry ingredients into mixing bowl. Combine egg and milk. Melt shortening, add to egg mixture. Add all at once to dry ingredients. Stir quickly until dry ingredients are moistened. Drop batter from tablespoon into well-greased muffin pans. Fill two thirds full. Bake at 400° for 25 minutes.

If you want to describe how a person usually makes muffins rather than telling them how to do it, you need to make several changes. First, the verb must be changed to the simple present tense by adding the third person singular -*s* form of the verb.

First, Katie sift*s* dry ingredients into mixing bowl.

Second, articles *(the, a, an)* must be added before the nouns.

First, Katie sifts *the* dry ingredients into *a* mixing bowl.

The following paragraph describes how Katie makes muffins. Complete it by adding the verb in the present tense form and adding the articles.

Katie likes to bake fresh muffins every Sunday morning. First, she _____

_____dry ingredients into _____mixing bowl, and _____

_____egg and milk. Then, she _____ _____shortening and

_____it to _____egg mixture. After that, she _____it all at

once to _____dry ingredients. Next, she _____it quickly until _____dry ingredients are moistened. She _____ _____

batter from _____tablespoon into well-greased muffin pans.

Finally, she _____ _____muffin pans two thirds full and _____

them at 400° for 25 minutes.

EXERCISE 1.3

grammatical focus: imperatives, third person singular -s, articles

The following directions describe how to get to Mike's house from the university campus. Notice that the imperative form of the verb is used and that some articles are omitted. Again the steps are numbered to help the reader easily follow the directions. Underline all the verbs in the imperative form.

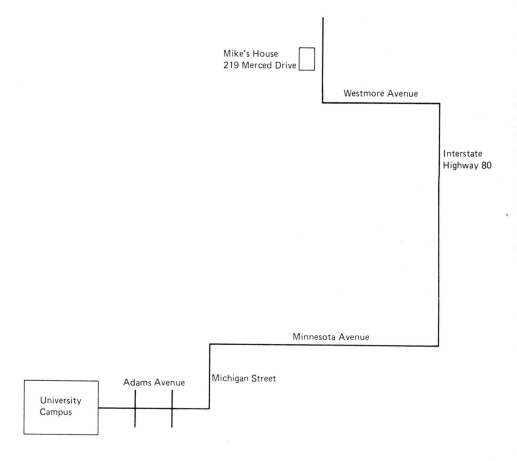

1. Drive down Adams for three blocks.
2. Turn left at Michigan.
3. At intersection of Minnesota, turn right and take Minnesota to Highway 80.
4. Go north on Highway 80 for two miles to Westmore exit.
5. Exit west on Westmore and drive for one mile.
6. Turn right at Merced. His house is at 219 Merced.

If you wanted to describe the route that Mike usually takes on his way home from the campus, you would need to change the form of the verb to the simple present tense and add the necessary articles. On a separate sheet of paper, rewrite each step as if you were describing how Mike typically goes home.

1. To get home from campus, Mike usually drives down Adams Avenue for three blocks.
2. He. . . .
3.
4.
5.
6.

EXERCISE 1.4

rhetorical focus: sentence connectors of chronological order

Very often a selection that describes how to do something includes sentence connectors that make the order of the steps clear. The following are common connectors for indicating a sequence of steps.

First,	After,	Next,
Second,	After that,	Then,
Third,	Afterwards,	Finally,

Notice that the expressions are followed by commas.
    Underline all the sentence connectors in the paragraphs on baking muffins (Exercise 1.2). Notice that it is not necessary to use a sentence connector with every sentence.

Other ways for indicating a sequence of steps are the following.

	first		need to	
The	second	thing	you have to	do is to cut the block of wood.
	next		should	

	first			
The	next	step		is to cut the block of wood.
	final			

With these patterns the infinitive form of the verb *to cut* is used rather than the imperative form, cut. Rewrite the sentences in the left column beginning with the phrase in the right column. Be sure to use the infinitive form of the verb and to add the necessary articles.

1. Remove fire extinguisher from wall.	1. The first thing you need to do is . . .
2. Combine egg and milk.	2. The next thing you have to do is . . .
3. Glue mirror on the block of wood.	3. The final step is . . .
4. Direct nozzle at base of flame.	4. The third step is . . .
5. Sift dry ingredients into mixing bowl.	5. To begin you need to . . .

EXERCISE 1.5

rhetorical focus: placement of adverbs

In describing a process, adverbs are often used to indicate how something should be done. For example, a recipe might state:

Thoroughly mix the batter.
OR
Mix the batter *thoroughly.*

Notice that the adverb could occur at the beginning of the sentence or after the object *(the batter).*

Sometimes the object is omitted but understood. For example, in the following sentence it is understood that what is added is the shortening even though this word is not included in the sentence.

Quickly add to the egg mixture.

In this type of sentence the adverb can be placed directly after the verb.

Add *quickly* to the egg mixture.

In the following sentences change the placement of the adverb from the beginning of the sentence to after the object, or to after the verb if the object is understood but omitted.

example:

Carefully insert the card.   Insert the card *carefully.*

1. Quickly remove the extinguisher from the wall.
2. Generously season with spices.
3. Carefully direct the nozzle at the base of the flame.
4. Securely glue the mirror on the block of wood.
5. Regularly water the seeds.
6. Thoroughly mix with the egg mixture.
7. Carefully thump the pot.
8. Gently smooth the soil surface.
9. Carefully combine with the dry ingredients.
10. Slowly simmer with the vegetables.

Reading Selection

What Effects Do Smog and Smoke Have on the Growth of Seedlings?

Plant five radish seeds in each of three small clay flowerpots filled with earth to a depth of about 5 cm. Water the seeds regularly and wait until leaves appear. Label the pots A, B, and C. Place each pot in a small dish.

Get two clear plastic bags (sandwich size will do) and two rubber bands. Cover pot B with a bag and fasten the bag in place with a rubber band.

Burning matches give off an unpleasant smoke. Take two wooden kitchen matches and stick them into the soil in pot C. Light a third match and use it to light the other two matches. While the matches are burning, carefully slip the second bag over the pot and fasten it in place with a rubber band. The matches will burn out quickly, leaving smoke in the air over the seedling.

Keep the pots on a window sill and water them regularly by pouring a small amount of water into the dishes in which they were placed. Observe the plants each day for at least three weeks and keep a log of your observations.

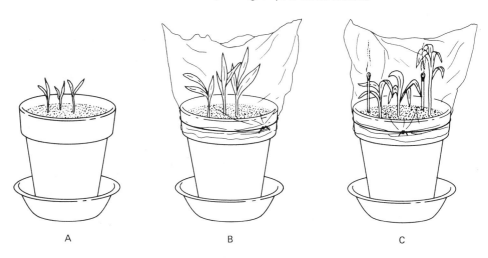

Observations	Week 1	Week 2	Week 3
Pot A			
Pot B			
Pot C			

(Source: Willard Jacobson et al., *Science: Generating Ideas*. New York: American Book Company, 1972, p. 180. Reprinted by permission of D. C. Heath.)

EXERCISE 1.6

The preceding passage gives the directions for an experiment to discover the effect of smog and smoke on the growth of young plants.

1. This selection, like the passage on making periscopes, lists the necessary equipment. What materials are needed for this experiment?

2. The passage makes frequent use of the imperative to indicate what needs to be done. Underline all the verbs in the imperative.

3. The selection also contains several adverbs to describe how the steps should be completed. Circle these adverbs.

4. No sentence connectors of chronological order are contained in the passage. Select three sentences from the reading and add sentence connectors to them.

Writing Tasks

☐ SITUATION ONE
   The Nurseryman

Assume that you work for a nursery. Many people ask you questions about the best way to transplant a plant.

☐ *TASK*

   Use the information on page 12 to write a paragraph description on how to transplant a plant. Include some of the following sentence connectors of chronological order in your description.

First,	Then,
Second,	After that,
The third thing you need to do,	Finally,

Be certain to add the articles wherever they are needed.

1. Remove plant and root ball from original container.

2. Cover drainage hole with pebbles and add some potting mixture.

3. Fill container with soil until root ball surface is near rim of container.

4. Center root ball and fill in sides with potting mix.

5. Thump pot carefully to settle potting mix.

6. Smooth soil surface gently with fingers.

(Adapted from Sunset Books, *How to Grow Houseplants*. Menlo Park, Cal.: Lane Publishing Company, 1975, p. 17.)

SITUATION TWO
The Bank Employee

Many banks now provide automatic banking machines so that an individual can bank at any time. In order to bank, an individual must have a transaction card and follow certain steps. The steps on page 13 are all necessary to receive cash. Try to put the steps in the correct order by placing a number before each. The first one is done for you.

_____Key in the amount of your transaction.

_____Follow the directions displayed on the machine.

_____The machine will double-check your entry. If it's shown correctly, press the

OK key.

___1___ Insert your card face down as shown on the machine.

_____As the directions indicate, key in your secret code number.

_____At the end of the transaction, take your receipt and keep it for your records.

☐ TASK

You are a bank employee and you want to tell a customer how to use the automatic banking machine. Complete the following letter in which you describe how to use the machine. Be sure to use the imperative form of the verb (*insert*) and sentence connectors such as *first, second, then, after that,* etc.

Dear Sir:

Using the automatic banking machine is quite easy. All you have to do is complete the following steps. First,

Sincerely,

☐ SITUATION THREE
The Librarian

The card catalog is a valuable tool in using a library because it lists all the books contained in that library by both author and subject. In order to use a card catalog, it is necessary to follow certain steps. See if you can put the steps listed below in proper order to indicate the procedure for checking the subject catalog under "Japan." The first one is done for you.

_____Find the subheading that you are interested in, such as "Japan-History" or

"Japan-Politics."

The correct order is 4, 2, 5, 1, 3, 6.

_____Copy down the name of the author, the title, and the call number.

___1___ Go to the subject catalog and look in the drawer labeled "Japan."

_____Go and search for the books in the stacks (the library shelves).

_____Select the book or books that you want to look at.

_____Consult the map of the library to find out where the book is located.

_____Check the book out.

☐ *TASK*

You are a librarian in a college library. You want to have a simple set of directions to give to new students on how to use the card catalog. Complete the paragraph below describing how to use a card catalog. Use the imperative and sentence connectors of chronological order.

The card catalog is an important tool for locating material in the library. In order to use a card catalog effectively, be sure to do the following things. First,

---

	JAPAN—POLITICS AND GOVERNMENT
DS	Borton, Hugh.
889	Japan since 1931, its political and social developments, by
B65	Hugh Borton ... New York, International secretariat, Insti-
	tute of Pacific relations, 1940.

     xii p., 2 1., 3-149 p. 23½cm. (I. P. R. inquiry series)

     "Bibliographical note": p. 131-137.

    1. Japan—Pol. & govt.   2. Japan—Soc. condit.   3. Japan-Econ. condit.—1918-   I. Title

     Library of Congress   DS889.B65   41-51526

—————Copy 2.

     Copyright   [8]   952.033

The correct order is 2, 4, 1, 6, 3, 5, 7.

SITUATION FOUR
The Chemistry Teacher

You want to illustrate for your class the necessary conditions for yeast plants to grow. You have devised a simple experiment to show them this.

☐ TASK

First, put the individual steps of the experiment in the correct order. Second, complete the following paragraph, in which you tell your students what they must do to determine the necessary conditions for yeast to grow. Be sure to use the imperative form of the verb and sentence connectors of chronological order.

_____Put a teaspoon of this yeast in a cup.

_____In two of the cups add warm water until the cup is one half full.

___1___Get a package of dry yeast.

_____Set all three cups aside for one half hour.

_____Examine all three cups to see what has happened.

_____Follow the same procedure in two other cups.

_____To one of the cups of water and yeast, add one teaspoon of sugar.

In order to determine the necessary conditions for yeast to grow, follow this simple experiment.

This experiment illustrates that for yeast to grow there must be _____

and _____.

The correct order is 2, 4, 1, 6, 7, 3, 5.

15

Peer Correction of Student Compositions

(1) A driver must take care in starting a parked car. (2) Before you begin, close all the doors and fasten securely your seat belt. (3) If you are starting from a parking space at curb, the first thing you need to do is to look for bicycles and vehicles approaching from rear. (4) Second, use your turn signal, but don't assume the other drivers have seen it. (5) Third, drive out slowly. (6) Remember you don't have the right of way. (7) If you are backing out of parking space, never guess that all is clear behind you. (8) First, before getting in vehicle, look behind it. (9) Second, after you are in the vehicle, don't rely on your rear view mirror. (10) Next, look back over your shoulder, keeping area behind your vehicle in view. (11) Finally, back out.

practice in correcting

The passage above describes how to start a car. It has several errors in it. Follow the instructions below and correct the compositions as directed.

Sentence 2: Correct the position of the adverb.

Sentence 3: Add the necessary articles.

Sentence 5: For variety, replace *Third* with another sentence connector.

Sentence 7: Add the necessary article.

Sentence 8: Do not use *first* because *before* indicates when you should do this step. Add the necessary article.

Sentence 9: Do not use *second* because *after* indicates when you should do this step.

Sentence 10: Add the necessary article.

Sentence 11 : Add an adverb to describe how you should back out.

2

Describing
an Object

The best way to describe the physical characteristics of an object is, of course, to point to the actual object or to show a picture of it. At times, however, it is not necessary or possible to include an illustration of the object. Instead a description of the important characteristics of the object such as its size, shape, and color is adequate. The description might then proceed to describe other characteristics of the object such as its purpose or construction.

EXERCISE 2.1

grammatical focus: the verb to be, *subject–verb agreement*

The verb *to be* is frequently used to describe an object. The following paragraph describes the planet Saturn. Underline all the forms of *to be* in the paragraph.

Saturn is similar in composition to Jupiter. Both planets are giant gas balls of hydrogen and helium with hot interiors. Both have dark-colored bands in their atmosphere. Saturn's unique feature is its ring system. Around its equator there are three flat rings, one inside the other and in the same plane. These rings are probably either pieces of rock or frozen gas.

A verb in English must agree in number with the subject of the sentence. In the paragraph on Saturn, connect each verb with its subject as in the following example.

(Saturn) (has) a smaller version of Jupiter's Great Red Spot.

Remember when a sentence begins with the word *there*, the subject will follow *to be*.

There (are) swirling (currents) in Saturn's atmosphere.

EXERCISE 2.2

grammatical focus: the verb to be, *subject–verb agreement*

Complete the following paragraph with a form of *to be*. Be sure to have the verb agree in number with the subject.

The Planets

There _____nine planets, including the Earth, in the solar system. Going outwards from the Sun, they _____Mercury, Venus, (Earth), Mars, Jupiter,

18

Saturn, Uranus, Neptune, and Pluto. They ＿＿＿＿＿＿＿very different in size and composition. Mercury, the planet closest to the Sun, ＿＿＿＿＿＿＿a scorching ball of rock not much bigger than the Moon. Jupiter, the biggest planet, ＿＿＿＿＿＿＿a gigantic ball of cold gas thirteen hundred times bigger than the Earth. And, of course, there ＿＿＿＿＿＿＿great differences in the planets' "years" (the time they take to circle the Sun) because of their different distances from the Sun. Funnily enough, the planets' "days" (the time they take to turn on their axis) ＿＿＿＿＿＿＿ shortest for the biggest planets.

The planets fall roughly into two groups, the *minor*, or *terrestrial* planets—that is, those that more or less resemble Earth—and the major planets, so-named because of their size. The terrestrial planets ＿＿＿＿＿＿＿Mercury, Venus, Mars, and Pluto. They have a hard rock core, like that of Earth. The major planets Jupiter, Saturn, Uranus, and Neptune ＿＿＿＿＿＿＿primarily gaseous. Other ways of grouping the planets ＿＿＿＿＿＿＿as *inner* and *outer* planets. The inner planets from Mercury to Mars form a natural unit in the solar system as far as distance is concerned. Then there ＿＿＿＿＿＿＿a comparatively large "gap" before we reach Jupiter and the outer planets. In this gap there ＿＿＿＿＿＿＿a great "ring" made up of lumps of rock and known as the *asteroid belt*.

(Source: Robin Kerrod, *Purnell's Concise Encyclopedia of Science*. Great Britain: Purnell and Sons Limited, 1974, p. 182.)

Now connect each form of *to be* with its subject as you did in the paragraph on Saturn.

EXERCISE 2.3

grammatical focus: the verb to be, *subject–verb agreement*

Complete the following description of the major parts of a plant. Be sure when you use the verb *to be* that it agrees in number with the subject. Notice that the description starts at the bottom of the plant and proceeds upward.

A plant consists of three major parts. They ＿＿＿＿＿＿＿the roots, the stem, and the leaves. The root system ＿＿＿＿＿＿＿composed of the

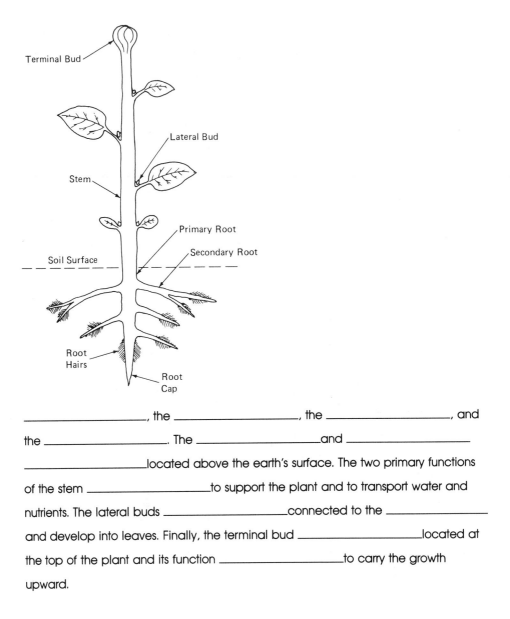

Terminal Bud

Lateral Bud

Stem

Primary Root

Secondary Root

Soil Surface

Root Hairs

Root Cap

_____, the _____, the _____, and

the _____. The _____and _____

_____located above the earth's surface. The two primary functions

of the stem _____to support the plant and to transport water and

nutrients. The lateral buds _____connected to the _____

and develop into leaves. Finally, the terminal bud _____located at

the top of the plant and its function _____to carry the growth

upward.

EXERCISE 2.4

mechanical focus: capitals, periods, commas with a series of items

A declarative sentence must begin with a capital and end with a period. Commas are used to separate several items joined by *and*. However, if there are only two items joined by *and*, no commas are used. Notice the punctuation in the following sentences.

The three major parts of a plant are the roots, the stem, and the leaves.
The stems and leaves are located above the earth's surface.

Add the necessary capitals, commas, and periods to the following description of an electric typewriter.

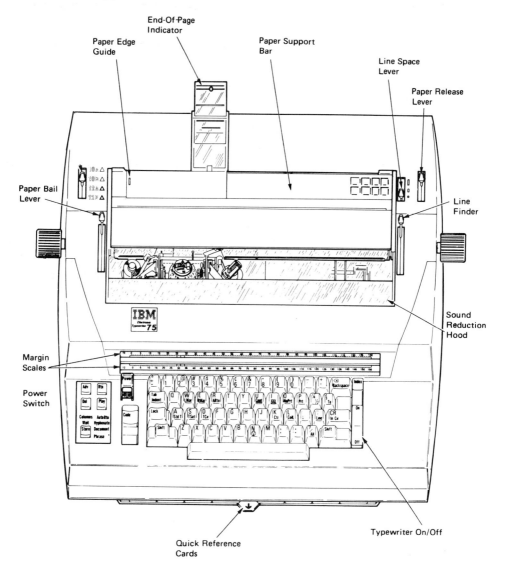

on the typewriter there are several features to aid in properly inserting the paper they are the paper bail lever the paper edge guide the end-of-page indicator and the paper support bar two devices for controlling the line spaces are the line space lever and the line finder the purpose of the sound reduction hood is to reduce the noise above the keyboard there are two margin scales one is for pica and the other is for elite on this machine the power switch is on the left and the on/off switch is on the right finally the quick reference cards are beneath the typewriter

Now circle all the verbs in the paragraph and connect them with their subject as you did in Exercise 2.1.

EXERCISE 2.5

rhetorical focus: descriptive nouns and adjectives of shape

You can sometimes describe objects by indicating their shape. The shape can be described in two ways:

As a noun: It's a rectangle.

As an adjective: It's rectangular.

Notice that an article (*a, an, the*) is used with the noun, but not with the adjective. Complete the following chart by describing the shape of the objects. You will find that a few shapes, such as a square, do not have a separate adjective form. In this case you can use "It's a square," or "It's square shaped."

example:	**noun**	**adjective**
	It's a rectangle.	It's rectangular.
1.		
2.		

example: noun   adjective

3.

4.

5.

6.

7.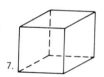

8.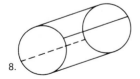

9.

EXERCISE 2.6

rhetorical focus: descriptive nouns and adjectives of shape

The flags pictured below are international alphabet code flags. Write a brief description of each flag. Use nouns and adjectives of shape and any of the following expressions: *there is/there are, contains, consists of, is composed of, is made up of.* Wherever possible indicate what the shapes resemble.

example:

A Y consists of diagonal stripes.
It resembles a candy cane.

Y

I

F

N

L

T

A

E

G

R

S

EXERCISE 2.7

rhetorical focus: descriptive nouns and adjectives of shape

Complete the description of the miter box pictured here by using adjectives and nouns of shape and the correct form of *to be*.

1. The Miter Box

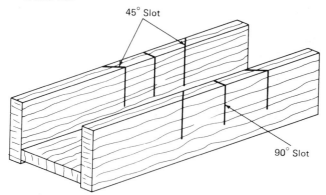

A miter box is used to guide a saw to cut squared ends.

It _____composed of three _____pieces of wood. There _____six slots to guide the saw in making a cut. Four of them _____ 45° slots and two of them _____90° slots. It resembles a napkin holder.

Write a brief description of the tools pictured below. Indicate the main parts of the tools by using any of the following expressions: *there is/there are, contains, consists of, is made up of, is composed of.* Be sure to describe the shape of the parts. You might also indicate what each part looks like.

2. A Round Knife

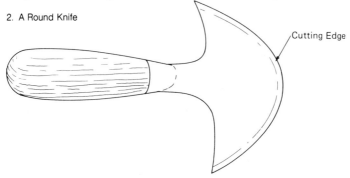

Cutting Edge

A round knife is used to cut leather.

_____

_____

3. A Plasterer's Trowel

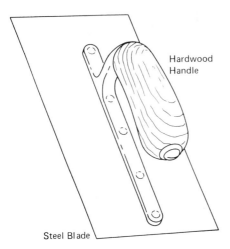

Hardwood
Handle

Steel Blade

A plasterer's trowel is used to apply plaster and to smooth the surface of the plaster.

_____

_____

Reading Selection

Get Your Bearings

Let's begin by looking at your compass dial. North, east, south and west are represented by N, E, S, and W. These cardinal points help interpret the language of degrees. Around the circular dial of your compass there are 360 degrees. Most compass dials are marked each 2 degrees, with a longer mark at each 10-degree interval. Beginning at N and reading clockwise, numerals indicate each 20 degrees, i.e., 20, 40, 60, etc. Note that north = both 0 and 360 degrees; east = 90 degrees; south = 180 degrees; west = 270 degrees. Since there is a 90-degree difference between these major points, you can see that to find, say, southeast—the midway point between 90 degrees (E) and 180 degrees (S)—you would add 45 degrees to 90 and come up with a reading of 135 degrees.

(Source: Reprinted from *Wildlife Country: How to Enjoy It*, page 86, copyright 1977 by the National Wildlife Federation.)

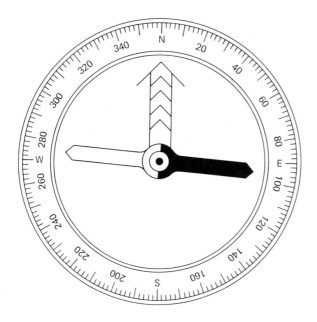

EXERCISE 2.8

When you describe an object, it is important to have a plan of organization. For example, if you were describing a typewriter, you might proceed from the top of the machine to the bottom; thus, you would start with the paper edge guide and end with the quick reference cards. Or you could describe each part as it is used by the typist; thus, you would begin with the power switch, then the on/off switch, then the paper guide, and so on. Notice the plan that is followed in the reading selection "Get Your Bearings."

1. The first sentence indicates where the author wishes to begin the description of the compass. Where does he start?
2. Further down the author describes the degrees on the compass. Where does this description begin? What order is followed in describing the degrees?
3. Notice that the description of the compass makes use of the verb *to be* and descriptive adjectives. Circle all the forms of *to be* in the paragraph. Circle the subject in these sentences. Finally, underline any descriptive adjectives of shape.

Writing Tasks

SITUATION ONE
The Astronomy Student

In your astronomy class your teacher is trying to demonstrate what led Aristotle to conclude that the Earth's surface is curved. She has asked you to investigate the shadows of the following objects and to summarize your findings in a paragraph.

☐ TASK

Study the objects pictured below and answer the following questions.

1. Which objects can cast a shadow shaped as a square?
2. Which objects can cast a shadow shaped as a triangle?
3. Which objects can cast a shadow shaped as a circle?
4. Which objects can cast a shadow shaped as a rectangle?
5. Which object can cast a shadow shaped *only* as a circle?

(Adapted from Roy Gallant and Isaac Asimov. *Ginn Science Program, Advanced Level A*, Teacher's Edition. Boston: Ginn and Company, 1973, p. 51.)

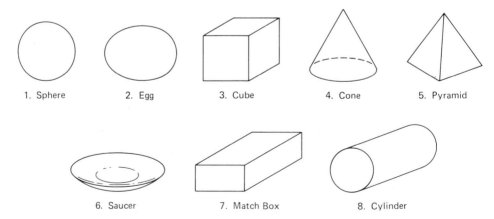

| 1. Sphere | 2. Egg | 3. Cube | 4. Cone | 5. Pyramid |

| 6. Saucer | 7. Match Box | 8. Cylinder |

Now complete the following paragraph using the verb *to be* and the names of shapes.

Correct answers: (1) 3, 5, 7 (2) 4, 5 (3) 1, 2, 4, 6, 8 (4) 3, 7 (5) 1

28

Aristotle believed that the earth was a _____ because it cast a

_____ shadow on the moon during an eclipse. The examples above

demonstrate that several objects can cast _____ shadows.

They _____ a _____ , a _____ , a _____ ,

a _____ , and a _____ . However, a _____

_____ the only object that can cast a shadow only as a _____ .

SITUATION TWO
The Music Teacher

You are a music teacher. You are writing a handbook on simple instruments that can be used with children. Accompanying each instrument is a brief description of its shape and the way it can be used.

☐ TASK

Write a brief description of the shape of the hand drum pictured below. Then complete the paragraph with some of the following information.

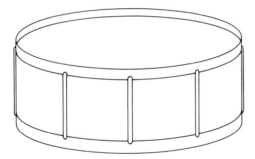

- The size of a hand drum varies from 10 inches to 24 inches in diameter.
- It is usually played with the hands, but mallets, brushes, or sand blocks can be used.
- It is a valuable tool to teach motor coordination.
- Large or heavy drums should not be used with children.

SITUATION THREE
The Physical Education Instructor

You are writing a text on beginning archery. One section deals with aiming the bow and arrow. In this section you want to include a description of the ring target.

Write a brief description of the ring target. The numbers in the circles indicate the scoring value of the circle. The color of each ring is listed on the side of the target.

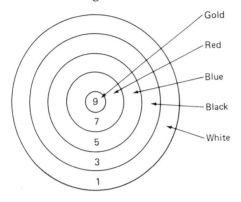

SITUATION FOUR
The Botanist

You are writing a book on how to identify edible mushrooms. As part of the book you are going to include a description of the major parts of a mushroom.

□ *TASK*

Use the diagram below to write a description of a mushroom. Start at the top of the mushroom and describe each part by using the following phrases.

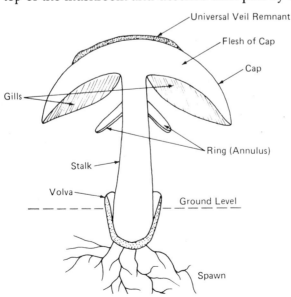

- At the top of
- Underneath the universal veil remnant
- The main support of the mushroom
- Beneath the ground level

Wherever possible use descriptive adjectives of shape. Be sure that the verb agrees in number with the subject.

SITUATION FIVE
The International Student

You are an international student. Your class is discussing the flags of various countries. Your teacher has asked you to write a brief description of the flag of your country.

TASK

Write a description of your country's flag (or if you are a resident of the United States, the flag of the country of your ancestors). Include a description of its colors and the objects it contains. If you are not familiar with the flag of your country, consult an encyclopedia. You might also indicate what the objects on the flag symbolize.

Peer Correction of Student Compositions

The following essay describes the windup tape measure pictured here.

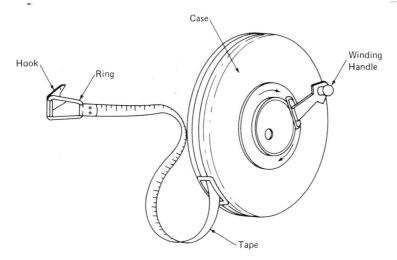

(1) A windup tape measure is an essential tool for carpenter. (2) It is composed a hook ring tape and winding handle. (3) The hook looks like two triangles attached to rectangle. (4) Next, the ring is trapezoid and is attached to the hook. (5) There are a tape connected to the ring. (6) This shows the measurements. (7) The tape is wound up in a case which is circle and has rough surface. (8) The winding handle is cylinder and is attached to case.

practice in correcting

The composition above has several errors in it. Follow the instructions below and correct the composition as directed.

Sentence 1: Add the necessary article.
Sentence 2: Add the necessary punctuation and preposition.
Sentence 3: Add the necessary article.
Sentence 4: Add the necessary article.
Sentence 5: Correct the error in subject–verb agreement.
Sentence 7: Correct the use of *circle*. Add the necessary article.
Sentence 8: Correct the use of *cylinder.* Add the necessary article.

3

Describing
a Place

As with an object, the best way to describe a place is to
show someone the actual place or to take a picture of it.
When this is not possible or necessary, a description
of the important characteristics of the place can be given.
If the place is a home or a room, it is important to
describe the size and arrangement of the space involved.
If, on the other hand, the place includes many buildings
such as a downtown area, the description will likely focus
on the location of the various buildings. Finally, if the place
is an entire country, the description will be much more
general and provide information about such things as the
land formation, climate, and major cities.

EXERCISE 3.1

grammatical focus: subject–verb agreement

The following passage describes the children's bedrooms and play area that are pictured below.

    The children's area in this house consists of three small sleeping rooms, a bathroom, a playroom, and a storage closet. Though the bedrooms are small, the high ceiling and many windows give a sense of spaciousness. In the storage closet there is a folding bed for overnight guests.

    The playroom contains a large cupboard for storing toys and games. It also has a bookcase and a table so the room can double as a study hall. In addition, the vinyl floors in the bedrooms and playrooms are easy to maintain.

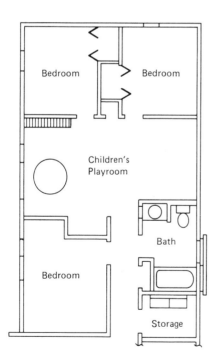

(Adapted from *Sunset Books, Children's Rooms and Play Yards*. Menlo Park, Cal.: Lane Publishing Company, 1976, p. 13.)

Notice that since the selection describes an area that now exists, all the verbs are in the present tense. Circle all the verbs in the passage and connect them with the subject or subjects in the following manner.

The children's (area) in this house (consists) of three small sleeping rooms, . . .

EXERCISE 3.2

grammatical focus: articles

Very often the article *a(n)* is placed before an object that has not been previously mentioned. If there is more than one object, a number may be used instead. On the other hand, *the* is used before items that have already been mentioned. In the following passage draw an arrow to connect all the numbered items with the first mention of the same item.

example:

The house has a large playroom. *The playroom* is located next to the kitchen.

The children's area in this house consists of three small sleeping rooms, a bathroom, a playroom, and a storage closet. Though *the bedrooms* are small, the high ceiling and many windows give a sense of spaciousness. In *the storage closet* there is a folding bed for overnight guests.

The playroom contains a large cupboard for storing toys and games. It also has a bookcase and a table so *the room* can double as a study hall. In addition, the vinyl floors in the *bedrooms* and *playroom* are easy to maintain.

EXERCISE 3.3

grammatical focus: articles

The following paragraph describes the floor plan of the apartment pictured here.

The floor plan of my house is very simple. The only complicated feature is that you have to walk upstairs to enter the house. If you stand at the top of the stairs and look straight ahead, you look into the bathroom. To the left of that is the kitchen. Beyond the kitchen is a back porch which is connected to the kitchen by a sliding glass door. There is a fireplace between the top of the stairs and the kitchen. On the near side of the fireplace is the living room.

At this point, it helps to leave the top of the stairs and go to the left. The first door leads to my bedroom. Inside is a large closet. Next to the first bedroom is another bedroom. This bedroom is connected to a study. It isn't necessary to walk in order to see into all the rooms in the house. You can see them all from the top of the stairs.

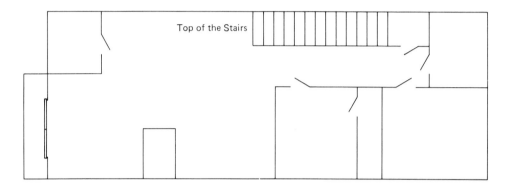

Top of the Stairs

First, label the rooms in the diagram above. Next, list the rooms and objects in the house that are first introduced with the article *a*, as, for example, *a fireplace*.

Now list all the rooms and objects in the house that are first introduced with the article *the*.

Quite often rooms that are common in the homes of a particular country are introduced with *the*. Why do you think a back porch, a sliding glass door, a fireplace, and a large closet are not introduced with *the*? Notice also that directions such as *the* top are also introduced with *the*. Underline all the directions that begin with *the*.

EXERCISE 3.4

grammatical focus: articles

Add *a(n)* or *the* to the following description of an American house. Remember to use *the* initially only with rooms that are common in American homes.

You enter this house, as you would most American homes, in _____living room. As you enter, _____dining room is directly in front of you and _____ kitchen is to the left of _____ dining room. Both _____ living room and

dining room open onto _____ deck. _____ master bedroom is to the right of

_____ living room. One of _____ bathrooms adjoins _____ master

bedroom. Two other bedrooms are in the farthest right-hand corner from _____

living room. Finally, there is _____ utility room between these two bedrooms and

_____ dining room.

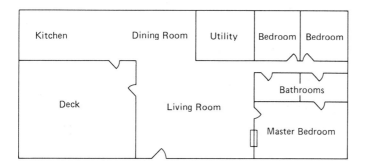

EXERCISE 3.5

grammatical focus: prepositions with expressions of place

Describing a floor plan or the location of buildings in a city often requires the use of prepositions. For example, in Exercise 3.3 the description of the apartment included expressions such as *at the top of, to the left of,* and *on the near side of.* The following sentences employ other expressions of place to describe the diagram of First Avenue and Main Street. Notice particularly the prepositions in these expressions.

The bakery is *next to* the post office.
The bakery is *adjacent to* the post office.
The bakery is *near* the post office.

The parking lot is *in back of* the bakery and the post office.
The parking lot is *behind* the bakery and the post office.
The post office and the bakery are *in front of* the parking lot.

The post office is *at the corner of* Main Street and First Avenue.
The post office is *on* Main Street.

The post office is *to the east of/to the right of* the bakery.
The post office is *in the center of* town.

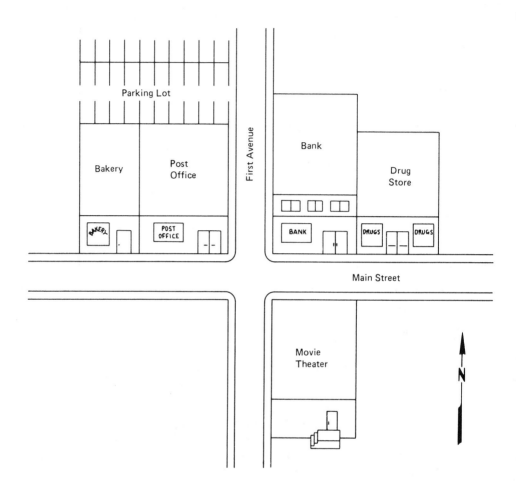

The movie theater is *kitty-cornered from* the post office.
The movie theater is *diagonally across from* the post office.
The movie theater is *across the street from* the bank.

The drugstore is *down the street from* the post office.

Write a one-sentence description of the buildings in downtown Centerville, pictured on page 39. Underline the expressions of place—for example, *the barber shop is <u>next to</u> the pool hall.* Try to use different expressions of location for each one.

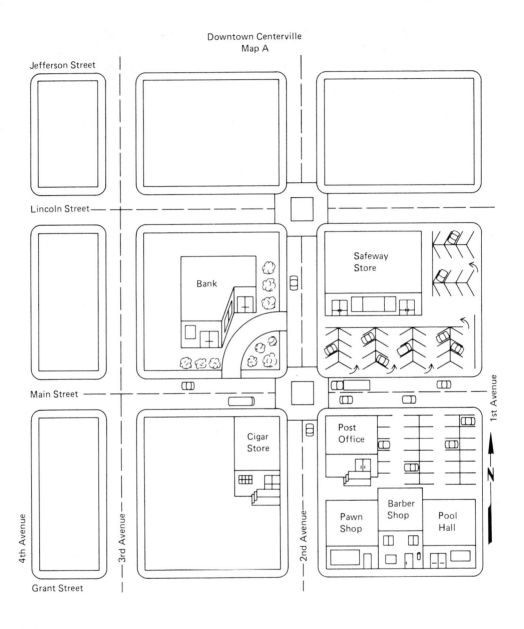

Downtown Centerville
Map A

1. Safeway _____

2. The bank _____

3. The barber shop / the pool hall _____

_____

4. The parking lot / the barber shop and the pool hall _____

_____

5. The pawn shop / the barber shop _____

_____

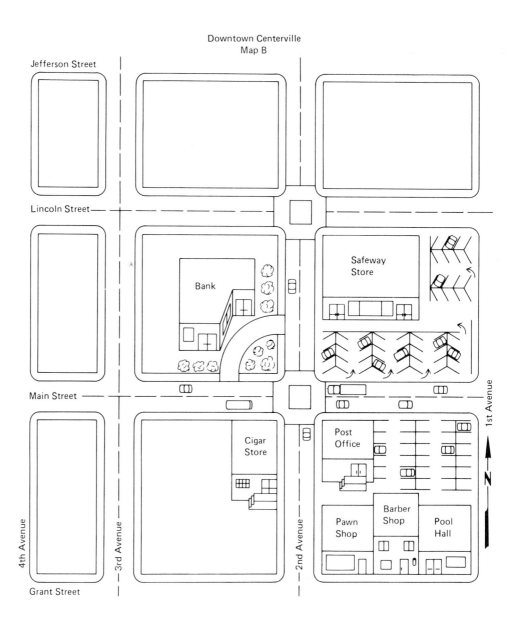

Downtown Centerville
Map B

6. The post office / the bank _____

_____

7. The cigar store / the post office _____

_____

8. The post office / the pawn shop _____

_____

Centerville is missing several important buildings. To make the downtown area complete, draw in the following buildings on map A: the movie theater, the hospital, the real estate agency, John's Grill, the law office, the courthouse, Lincoln High School, and the drugstore.

Next, write a one-sentence description of the location of each of these buildings.

Finally, describe to a partner the location of each building you have added. Have your partner draw in on map B the location of your buildings.

EXERCISE 3.6

rhetorical focus: descriptive adjectives

Using specific details and descriptive words helps a reader to form a picture of the particular place that is being described. The following sentences describe various locations in San Francisco. In each sentence underline the descriptive adjective.

example:

San Francisco has a temperate climate.
(Be sure to look up the meaning of any words you are not familiar with.)

1. San Francisco is a compact and compelling city with many spectacular views.
2. The wide assortment of nationalities that live in San Francisco make it a cosmopolitan city.
3. North Beach, San Francisco's Italian community, is a region of excellent restaurants and lively night life.
4. Chinatown is a bustling and colorful area dotted with import and curio shops.
5. Fisherman's Wharf is a world-famous tourist attraction of sidewalk seafood stalls and restaurants.

6. Ghirardelli Square is a remodeled red-brick complex of intriguing shops, art galleries, and fine restaurants.
7. San Francisco's financial district is filled with impressive office buildings.
8. Golden Gate Park, a renowned metropolitan park, is crisscrossed with tree-lined walks, bridle paths, and bicycle trails.
9. Coit Tower, a well-known landmark, provides a spectacular view of the city.
10. Japan Center is a string of handsome white buildings of showrooms, shops, and restaurants.

Complete the following paragraph on San Francisco with descriptive adjectives. Try to use adjectives other than the ones used above.

San Francisco is a _____and _____city. Along

with a _____climate, San Francisco offers _____

attractions. Perhaps, the most famous is Golden Gate Park, a _____

park. Another landmark is Coit Tower with its _____view of the city.

For those who like to browse, Chinatown is filled with _____shops; in

addition, Ghirardelli Square provides a wide variety of _____shops.

For those who enjoy night life, North Beach with its _____night life

and Fisherman's Wharf with its _____restaurants are a must. Just

strolling along San Francisco's _____streets is a _____

experience.

Reading Selection

The Swahili Home

A common style of home in the coastal cities of Tanzania is what is sometimes
called the Swahili house. To the outsider, *the* house looks like a small single-family
dwelling, rectangular in shape with a single door in the middle of the front of the
house. When one enters *the* door, however, he looks down a long hallway often with
three doors opening on each side of *the* corridor. In each of these six rooms, usually,
there is a family; as many as six families, often from fifteen to twenty-five people, live

in this single house. At the rear of *the* home there is a common area for cooking, with

another area for a toilet and possibly a place for bathing as well.

(Source: John Condon and Fathi Yousef. *An Introduction to Intercultural Communication.* Indianapolis: Bobbs-Merrill Educational Publishing, 1975, p. 154.)

EXERCISE 3.7

1. In describing a room, it is important to have a plan for organizing the paragraph. How does this paragraph begin? How is the remainder of the paragraph organized?

2. This, and most descriptions of places that still exist, are written in the present tense. Thus, it is important that the verb agree in number with its subject. Connect all the verbs in the paragraph with their subject. Be careful with sentences with compound subjects.

3. When an object is first mentioned, the article *a(n)* is generally used. The next time the object is mentioned, *the* is used. Draw an arrow from the italicized examples of *the* to the first mention of that object. Why is *the* used with *front* and *middle?*

4. The paragraph makes use of prepositions and descriptive adjectives to make clear the location of the rooms and their characteristics. Underline all the descriptive adjectives in the paragraph. Circle all the expressions of place.

Writing Tasks

SITUATION ONE
The Real Estate Agent

You are a real estate agent. You are trying to sell the condominium pictured on page 44. You have decided to write a one-paragraph description of the condominium to use in your advertising.

TASK

Use the floor plan pictured on page 44 to complete the following paragraph.

This condominium is ideal for a ———————————————————————.

It includes a ——————————————————————. As you enter the

foyer, the kitchen is to your left.

(Now finish the description by describing the location of the dining area, the balcony, the living room, the den, the master bedroom, the full bath, the half bath, and the utility room.)

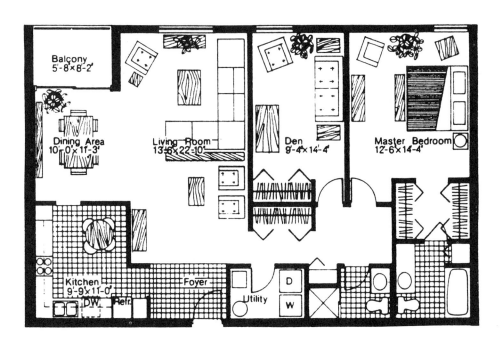

SITUATION TWO
The Hotel Manager

You are a hotel manager. You want to advertise the advantages of your hotel as a conference site. In your brochure about the hotel you have decided to include one paragraph on the conference space that you have available in the hotel.

☐ *TASK*

Write a one-paragraph description of the floor plan shown on page 45. Describe the location of the ballroom, the foyer, and the meeting rooms. Use the descriptive adjectives of shape from Chapter 2 and expressions of place.

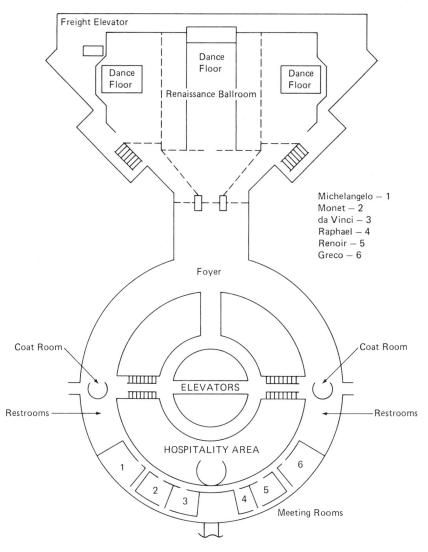

RENAISSANCE LEVEL

Freight Elevator

Dance Floor

Dance Floor

Renaissance Ballroom

Dance Floor

Michelangelo — 1
Monet — 2
da Vinci — 3
Raphael — 4
Renoir — 5
Greco — 6

Foyer

Coat Room

Coat Room

ELEVATORS

Restrooms

Restrooms

HOSPITALITY AREA

1
2
3
4
5
6

Meeting Rooms

THE RENAISSANCE CENTER — DETROIT, MICHIGAN

SITUATION THREE
The College Student

You are a college student. You are living away from home. Since your parents have not seen where you are living, they would like to know what it is like.

☐ *TASK*

Write a letter to your parents and describe the place where you are now living. If you are staying in an apartment or a home, describe the arrangement of the rooms. If you are staying in a dormitory, describe the objects in your room and the arrangement of these objects.

☐ SITUATION FOUR
The Travel Agent

You are a travel agent from the city of Eden. You want to have a brief description of the major attractions of Eden to distribute to various travel agencies.

☐ *TASK ONE*

First, add a descriptive adjective to each of the items listed below. Then use these phrases to write a description of Eden's main attractions.

_____ climate

_____ beaches

_____ scenery

_____ shops

_____ night life

_____ restaurants

_____ hotels

_____ festivals

_____ museums

☐ *TASK TWO*

One of Eden's most popular tourist attractions is Old Town. Some of Old Town's most frequented spots are: Bill's Salon, The Stagecoach Inn, The Old Post Office, The Gold Rush Museum, The Sawmill, The Jail, and The Steam Depot. Begin by drawing these places on the map of Old Town. (Be sure to add the names of the streets.) Then write a brief description of the location of these attractions to include in your brochure.

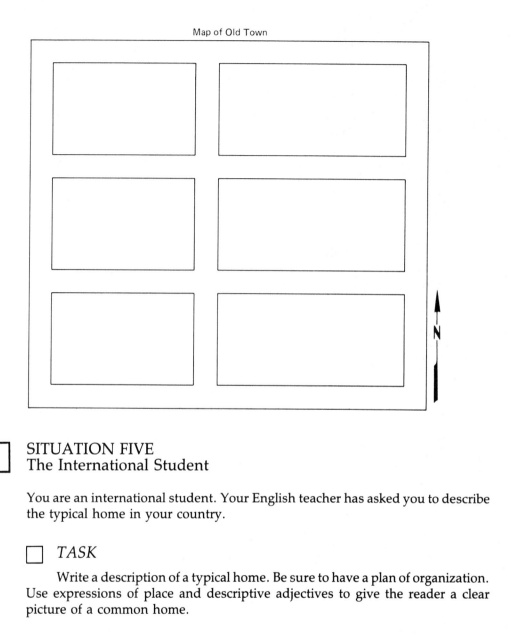

Map of Old Town

SITUATION FIVE
The International Student

You are an international student. Your English teacher has asked you to describe the typical home in your country.

☐ TASK

Write a description of a typical home. Be sure to have a plan of organization. Use expressions of place and descriptive adjectives to give the reader a clear picture of a common home.

Peer Correction of Student Compositions

The following essay describes how the large basement pictured here can be changed into three bedrooms and a play area.

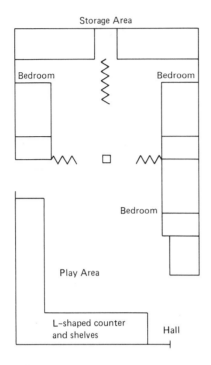

Storage Area

Bedroom

Bedroom

Bedroom

Play Area

L-shaped counter
and shelves

Hall

(1) Folding doors can transform a large basement into a children's area. (2) One area consist of two small bedrooms. (3) Each of these rooms have a bed and a big storage area. (4) Many toys, games, clothes, and sheets can be put to the storage area. (5) The other area consist of the bedroom and play area. (6) The play area is the side where there are an L-shaped counter and shelves. (7) Children can study and play at a counter, and many books and magazines can be stored into the shelves. (8) The bed is kitty-cornered of the counter and adjacent from one of the other beds. (9) A hall is the right side of the play area.

practice in correcting

The above composition has several errors in it. Follow these instructions and correct the composition as directed.

Sentence 2: Correct the error in subject–verb agreement.
Sentence 3: Correct the error in subject–verb agreement.

Sentence 4: Correct the error in the choice of preposition.

Sentence 5: Correct the error in subject–verb agreement and choice of article.

Sentence 6: Correct the error in subject–verb agreement and supply the missing preposition.

Sentence 7: Correct the error in the choice of article and preposition.

Sentence 8: Correct the errors in the choice of preposition.

Sentence 9: Supply the missing preposition.

4

Describing
a Personality

Biographies and autobiographies tell a story of an individual. Each individual, however, is so complex that not even an entire book can tell us everything about that person. Since there is so much that can be said about an individual, any description of a person will be limited. Often, of course, we want or need to know only some specific information about an individual. For example, an employer for a sales company clearly wants to know whether or not an individual is an aggressive salesperson. He probably is not concerned with whether or not this individual is an excellent musician or a good cook. As an employer, he primarily wants to know things about people that demonstrate whether or not they are good salespersons. The focus of this chapter is on describing one characteristic of an individual and providing specific details that illustrate that characteristic.

EXERCISE 4.1

grammatical focus: past tense

If a writer wants to describe a person who is living, he will, of course, use the present tense (e.g., "The President is a man of infinite energy"). If, however, the writer were writing a biography of this president after his death, he would use the past tense (e.g., "The President was a man of infinite energy"). The following passage describes Warren Harding (President of the United States from 1921 to 1923). It is written as if it were the year 1921.

Warren Harding has two great assets. First, he looks as a President of the United States should. He is superbly handsome. His face and carriage have a Washingtonian nobility and dignity, and he photographs well. He is also the friendliest man to enter the White House. He seems to like everybody. He wants to do favors for everyone and to make everyone happy. His affability is not merely the forced affability of a cold-blooded politician; it is transparently and touchingly genuine.

(Source: Adapted from page 126 in *Only Yesterday* by Frederick Lewis Allen. Copyright 1931 by Frederick Lewis Allen. Renewed, 1959, by Agnes Rogers Allen. Reprinted by permission of Harper & Row, Publishers, Inc.)

Rewrite the passage so it is appropriate for today. Change all the verbs to the past tense.

EXERCISE 4.2

grammatical focus: pronoun reference

When you use a pronoun, it is important to let the reader know who or what the pronoun refers to. For example, suppose you read the following sentences: *He has two great assets. He is superbly handsome. He seems to like everybody.* You would, of course, want to know who *he* refers to. Once the writer changes the first sentence to *Warren Harding has two great assets*, it is clear whom *he* refers to.

In Exercise 4.1 underline all the personal pronouns *(he, him, his)* that refer to Harding.

EXERCISE 4.3

The following passage was written by the store manager of a Safeway store. It describes two cashiers of the store, Nick Kremer and Alice Chen. The paragraph explains the manager's reasons for transferring one of these employees to another Safeway store. Fill in all of the blanks with either the names of these two employees or personal pronouns.

_____and _____both began working at my store during the summer of 1981. Initially, _____were very good friends. However, after a few weeks it was clear that _____had very different views on how to handle customers. _____was a very affable person and enjoyed talking with each of the customers. On the other hand, _____was very efficient. _____believed that as a cashier, _____had the responsibility to serve the customers quickly and efficiently. _____did not like the fact that _____chatted with each customer since this took time and often caused other customers to wait in line. One evening _____told _____that _____should not spend so much time talking to each customer. _____replied that the customers liked this. Furthermore, _____had no right to tell _____how to treat the customers. This led to an argument in the store. Eventually, I decided that it would be best for all concerned if _____did not work at the same store. Therefore, I transferred _____to the downtown Safeway store where _____is now happily employed.

EXERCISE 4.4

grammatical focus: expressions of quantity with count and noncount nouns

Describing a person often involves listing his or her characteristics. Sometimes these characteristics are nouns (_patience, gentleness, affability_). Since qualities are noncount, they must be preceded by the indefinite article _some_ or by any of the following quantity expressions: *(a) little, much, a lot of, a great deal of, a lack of.* For example:

The secretary shows *a great deal of* diligence.

In negative sentences noncount nouns can be preceded by the following expressions: *any, much, a lot of, a great deal of.* For example:

The secretary doesn't show *any* diligence.

The following individuals all work for Appleby Computers. Their supervisors are involved in writing up their work evaluations. Complete the sentences describing each of these individuals by adding a quantity expression. Keep the verb in the present tense and make sure it agrees in number with the subject. Make some of the sentences negative. For example:

Philomena Chan / exhibit / friendliness toward co-workers.
Philomena Chan exibits a great deal of friendliness toward co-workers.
    OR
Philomena Chan doesn't exhibit a great deal of friendliness toward co-workers.

1. Cathy Alvarez / show / diligence on the job.
2. Joe Davies and Ann White / demonstrate / leadership among their co-workers.
3. Bob Judge / exhibit / affability toward his fellow workers.
4. Dorleen Mo / have / creativity in marketing.
5. Jill Benson / show / willingness to assume responsibility.
6. Tsung-Su Wu / demonstrate / initiative in his position.
7. Ed Brennan and Mike Brown / exhibit / laziness.
8. Masahiko Akita / demonstrate / perseverance in his new position.
9. Lorraine Beale / exhibit / carelessness in her work.
10. Bob Brooks / demonstrate / dedication to the firm.

EXERCISE 4.5

grammatical focus: nonrestrictive relative clauses

mechanical focus: commas with nonrestrictive relative clauses

Two short sentences about an individual can be combined into one sentence by using a relative clause (a clause that modifies a noun). When a relative clause is used to add information about an individual who has already been identified, it must have commas around it. This type of a clause is called a *nonrestrictive clause*. Notice how the following sentences can be combined by replacing Warren Harding with *who* and placing commas around the clause.

Warren Harding was an affable man. Warren Harding was president from 1921 to 1923.

1. Warren Harding, who was an affable man, was president from 1921 to 1923.
2. Warren Harding, who was president from 1921 to 1923, was an affable man.

The information in the main clause receives the most emphasis. Thus, the first sentence emphasizes when Harding was president whereas the second sentence emphasizes that he was an affable man.

Use a relative clause to add the information listed below to the sentences you wrote in Exercise 4.4. In the first four sentences emphasize where the employee works. In the remainder of the sentences emphasize the information in Exercise 4.4. Be certain to use commas with the relative clauses.

example:

Philomena Chan exhibits a great deal of friendliness toward co-workers.
Philomena Chan joined the company three years ago.
Philomena Chan, who exhibits a great deal of friendliness toward co-workers, joined the company three years ago.

1. Cathy Alvarez works in the clerical division.
2. Joe Davies and Ann White are in finances.
3. Bob Judge is in personnel.
4. Dorleen Mo works in sales.
5. Jill Benson completed her master's degree in computer science.
6. Tsung-Su Wu came to the company from Control Data.
7. Ed Brennan and Mike Brown are frequently late for work.
8. Masahiko Akita was recently promoted.
9. Lorraine Beale has taken many sick days.
10. Bob Brooks was previously with IBM.

EXERCISE 4.6

rhetorical focus: descriptive adjectives of human characteristics

Descriptive adjectives are often used to describe a person. For example, suppose you were describing a relative who spends money unwisely. You might write, "My uncle is extravagant." Most likely you reached this conclusion because you witnessed many occasions on which he spent money foolishly. Perhaps you saw him overtip a waiter or buy a very expensive gift. If you want to convince someone that your uncle is extravagant, merely saying that he is a spendthrift is not enough. It is important to describe specific things he does that demonstrate he spends money unwisely.

The supervisor at Appleby Computers who wrote that Lorraine Beale is careless in her work probably based this conclusion on specific things that Lorraine did at work. Perhaps she frequently misplaces files or turns in work with many typographical errors. While she may be on time to work all the time and take very few sick days, these facts do not affect the conclusion that she is a careless worker.

This and the following exercises deal with the use of relevant details to support a generalization about a person.

The nouns listed below could all be used by a supervisor to describe a worker. In writing a work evaluation report a supervisor could write: "Bob Brooks demonstrates dedication to the firm." He could also use the adjective form: "Bob Brooks is a *dedicated* young man." List the adjective forms of the following characteristics. The first one is done for you.

noun	adjective
1. affability	affable
2. aggressiveness	
3. carefulness	
4. cooperation	
5. creativity	
6. dedication	
7. diligence	
8. enthusiasm	
9. independence	
10. industriousness	

noun	adjective
11. intelligence	
12. laziness	
13. patience	
14. perseverance	
15. punctuality	
16. responsibility	
17. self-sufficiency	
18. shyness	
19. sloppiness	
20. tardiness	

EXERCISE 4.7

rhetorical focus: relevancy of support

The following sentences describe specific things done by various employees of Appleby Computers. For each sentence, list the descriptive adjective that best describes this type of behavior. The first one is done for you. In some cases more than one adjective may be appropriate.

fact	characteristic
1. Philomena Chan has never been late for work.	punctual
2. Cathy Alvarez designed a more efficient way to file reports.	
3. Joe Davies has been invited to the homes of most of his fellow employees.	

fact   characteristic

4. Ann White usually comes to work for a few hours on Saturday morning.

5. Bob Judge submitted an important report with coffee stains on the paper.

6. Dorleen Mo usually eats lunch alone.

7. Jill Benson has been late to work six times in the past month.

8. Tsung-Su Wu has worked for six weeks on the financial report.

9. Ed Brennan asked his supervisor for a raise after being with the company for two months.

10. Mike Brown never offers to do any additional work.

11. Masahiko Akita was quite willing to share his typewriter when the office was short on equipment.

12. Lorraine Beale rarely asks her co-workers for their opinions when she is writing a report.

13. Bob Brooks will often spend two or three hours with new employees answering their questions about employee benefits.

EXERCISE 4.8

rhetorical focus: relevancy of support

List three of the characteristics in Exercise 4.6 that you feel describe your work habits.

1.

2.

3.

For each characteristic, list two things you have done either as a student or employee, which you think demonstrates that you are that kind of person. For example, if you believe you are punctual, you might indicate how many times you have been late for class or work in the last month.

characteristic one:

Fact One:

Fact Two:

characteristic two:

Fact One:

Fact Two:

characteristic three:

Fact One:

Fact Two:

Reading Selection

The following passage is taken from *Farewell to Manzanar*, the autobiography of Jeanne Wakatsuki Houston. The novel describes her experiences as a member of a Japanese-American family in the United States during the Second World War. In the following paragraph the author describes her father's idealism.

In those days *he* was a headstrong idealist. *He* was spoiled, the way eldest
sons usually are in Japan, used to having *his* way and he did not like what he saw
happening to the family. Ironically, it foreshadowed just the sort of thing he himself
would be faced with later on: too many children and not enough money. *His* father's
first wife bore five children. When *she* died, *he* remarried and four more came along.
His father, who had been a public official, ended up running a "teahouse" in
Hiroshima—something like a cabaret. It was a living, but Papa wanted no part of this.
In the traditional Japanese class system, samurai ranked just below nobility; then
came farmers and those who worked the land. Merchants ranked fourth, below the
farmers. For Papa, at seventeen, it made no difference that times were hard; the
idea of a teahouse was an insult to the family name. What's more, *their* finances
were in such a state that even as eldest son there was almost nothing for *him* to look
forward to. The entire area around Hiroshima, mainly devoted to agriculture, was
suffering a severe depression. In 1886 Japan had for the first time allowed its citizens
to emigrate and thousands from *his* district had already left the country in search of
better opportunities. Papa followed *them*.

(Source: From *Farewell to Manzanar* by Jeanne Wakatsuki Houston and James D. Houston. Copyright © 1973 by James D. Houston. Reprinted by permission of Houghton Mifflin Company.)

gloss

foreshadow: to suggest something before it happens
cabaret: a restaurant providing short programs of live entertainment

EXERCISE 4.9

1. Since the author wrote this description after her father's death, many of the verbs are in the past tense. Underline all the verbs in the simple past tense.
2. The paragraph contains many personal pronouns. For each of the numbered pronouns, list the noun that it refers to.

    1. he   the author's father

    2. he   _____

3. his _____

4. his _____

5. she _____

6. he _____

7. their _____

8. him _____

9. his _____

10. them _____

Writing Tasks

SITUATION ONE
The Film Critic

You are a film critic. You are writing a review of a recent film festival of Charlie Chaplin movies. You intend to include one paragraph in your review that focuses not on Chaplin's success, but rather on his personal hardships as a child.

☐ TASK

Use the information listed below to write one paragraph about the hardships of Chaplin's childhood. Begin by selecting those facts that demonstrate his hardships. Then decide on a logical order in which to present them. Be sure to keep the verb in the past tense and use pronoun reference. You might begin your paragraph with the following generalization: "Although Chaplin's success as an actor and director are well known, many people are not aware of his unhappy childhood."

facts:

1. Though Chaplin lived in the United States for over forty years, he never became an American citizen.
2. When Chaplin was quite young, his mother sued his father for nonsupport.
3. Chaplin, a British film comedian, director and producer, was born in London in 1889.
4. Because of their poverty, Chaplin, his mother, and his brother Sydney entered the Lambeth Workhouse.

5. After spending several years at Hanwell, Chaplin discovered that his mother had been sent to the Cane Hill lunatic asylum.

6. At Lambeth, Chaplin's family was separated; his mother went to the women's ward and he and his brother went to the children's ward.

7. Chaplin came to the United States in 1910 and soon began performing in motion picture comedies.

8. Chaplin's father died of alcoholic excess.

9. After three weeks at the Lambeth Workhouse, Chaplin and his brother were sent to the Hanwell School for Orphans and Destitute Children.

10. Chaplin's characterization of the little tramp made him world famous.

SITUATION TWO
The International Student

You are an international student. Your English teacher has asked you to write a character sketch of someone who is no longer living who has influenced your life. This person can be someone you knew personally or someone you have read about.

☐ TASK

Write one paragraph of the assigned character sketch. Be sure that this paragraph deals with only one aspect of this person's personality and include several specific facts that illustrate this characteristic. Keep the verbs in the past tense and use pronoun reference.

SITUATION THREE
The Prospective Employee

You are looking for employment. You have completed an application form for a position that you are quite interested in. Part of the application asks that you describe your work habits.

☐ TASK

Write a description of your work habits. Select one characteristic that you believe best describes your work habits such as responsibility, diligence, or carefulness. Include several specific things you have done that demonstrate this characteristic. Use the first person pronoun and keep the verbs in the present tense.

SITUATION FOUR
The Computer Company Supervisor

You are a supervisor at Appleby Computers. Part of your job requires that you write annual work evaluations of your employees.

☐ TASK

Select one of the Appleby employees described in Exercise 4.4 and write one paragraph of this individual's work evaluation report. Use the characteristic that is listed in Exercise 4.4 as your generalization but include several specific incidents that illustrate this characteristic. Be sure to combine short sentences by using relative clauses.

Peer Correction of Student Compositions

The International Student

(1) My grandmother was a very generous woman. (2) I can never forget her. (3) She always show friendliness and is very glad to help people who needed it. (4) For example, I remember one day she take me to her friend's house with lot of food and give it all to them because they were poor. (5) Furthermore, she was very diligent. (6) Her work is never done. (7) Sometimes, she cook Chinese food and sent it to her neighbor who was very sick and couldn't do anything. (8) She go to her house every day in order to help her cook dinner, clean a house, and go shopping. (9) She was died in 1968, but it seems to me she still lives in my heart. (10) I can see she was looking at me with smile when I helped someone. (11) She influenced me so much that I will remember her forever.

practice in correcting

The composition above has several errors in it. Follow these instructions and correct the composition as directed.

Sentence 3: Correct the errors in verb tense. Add an expression of quantity before friendliness.

Sentence 4: Correct the errors in verb tense and add the necessary article.

Sentence 6: Correct the error in verb tense.

Sentence 7: Correct the error in verb tense.

Sentence 8: Correct the error in verb tense and the use of the article.

Sentence 9: Correct the error in verb tense.

Sentence 10 : Correct the errors in verb tense and the use of the article.

The paragraph begins by stating that the grandmother was a very generous woman. Some of the sentences in the paragraph, however, do not support this generalization. List the sentences that do not directly support the idea that she was a generous women.

5

Describing an Event

In describing an event it is important to indicate the order in which things occurred. One way to make this sequence clear is the choice of verb tense and connecting devices such as *before, after,* and *while.* Sometimes writers describe an event as objectively as possible and do not include any of their own feelings. At other times, particularly when writers describe events that they themselves experienced, they include their own feelings. This chapter is devoted to describing personal events as well as public and scientific events.

EXERCISE 5.1

grammatical focus: verb tense: past progressive, past perfect

Describing an event that has already occurred frequently involves the use of three verb tenses.

- PAST TENSE: The driver of the truck *crashed* into a Ford Mustang.
- PAST PROGRESSIVE: As the driver *was making* a left turn, he crashed into a Ford Mustang.
- PAST PERFECT: The police reported that the truck driver *had been* negligent.

Notice that the past progressive is formed by using the past tense of *be (was)* as the auxiliary and the *-ing* form of the main verb *(making)*. The past perfect is composed of the past tense of *have (had)* as the auxiliary and the past participle of the main verb *(been)*.

The following passage is taken from the employee file of Charles McLaughlin, a truck driver for Loomis armored cars. It describes an accident he had while on duty.

(1) On March 13, while on duty, Charles McLaughlin, a driver employed by Loomis armored cars, was involved in an accident. (2) The accident occurred in Riverside, California. (3) As Mr. McLaughlin was turning right on Main and 33rd, he collided with a Volkswagen Rabbit. (4) This caused minor damage to the truck and serious damage to the car. (5) On the basis of the police report, the Loomis accident committee determined that Mr. McLaughlin had been careless. (6) As a result of the committee's conclusion, the branch manager reported that he had talked with Mr. McLaughlin about his driving record.

Notice that while most of the verbs are in the past tense, the past progressive and past perfect are also used. Underline the verb in the past progressive. Circle the two verbs in the past perfect.

The past progressive and past perfect are frequently used when two events in the past are described in the same sentence. In sentence 5, two events in the past are reported:

1. The accident committee determined something.

2. Mr. McLaughlin was careless.

What two events are described in sentence 6?

1.

2.

What two events are described in sentence 3?

1.

2.

EXERCISE 5.2

grammatical focus: verb tense: past progressive, past perfect

The following passage is also taken from the personnel file of Charles Mc-Laughlin. It describes two other accidents in which Mr. McLaughlin was involved. Fill in the blanks with the most appropriate verb tense. Use the past, past progressive, or past perfect tense.

On May 6, when Mr. McLaughlin _____ from his shift, he

(return)
_____ a roll-up door at the Loomis facility in Vallejo, causing

(run into)
significant damage to the door. Damage to the truck, however, _____

(be)
minor. Finally, on June 7, Mr. McLaughlin _____

(knock down)
several mailboxes near the edge of the company parking lot. There _____

(be)
damage to the mailboxes and minor paint damage to the truck.

The branch manager, David Rossi, _____ that he

(state)
_____ with Mr. McLaughlin on several occasions about his driving

(speak)
record. Mr. Rossi _____ that he _____

(add)   (warn)
Mr. McLaughlin that three preventable accidents in one year could lead to his

discharge.

EXERCISE 5.3

grammatical focus: adverbial clauses of time

mechanical focus: commas with adverbial clauses of time

Two sentences that describe an event in the past can often be combined by using an adverb of time such as *when, while, after, before,* or *as.* For example, the following two sentences can be combined by using the adverb *when.*

> I got there.
> The fire was on the Keno scoreboard.

> When I got there, the fire was on the Keno scoreboard.
> The fire was on the Keno scoreboard when I got there.

Notice that when the adverbial clause *(When I got there,)* is at the beginning of the sentence, a comma is used.

The following sentences all describe a fire in a Las Vegas hotel. Combine the sentences by using the adverb that is listed. If you begin the sentence with an adverbial clause, be sure to use a comma. Wherever possible, replace nouns with an appropriate pronoun the second time they are mentioned.

1. *while*
   Mr. Osbee was cooking.
   Mr. Osbee noticed the flames.
2. *after*
   The fire started in an attic above the hotel delicatessen.
   Strong drafts caused the fire to spread quickly.
3. *when*
   The smoke started seeping into the hotel rooms.
   Many guests were asleep.
4. *when*
   The commotion began.
   Many guests ran for the door.
5. *as*
   Many guests broke their windows.
   Many guests were faced with billowing smoke.
6. *after*
   Many guests rushed for the stairwells.
   Many guests found the stairwells blocked.

7. *while*
   One guest was looking frantically for an exit.
   The guest's wife collapsed.

EXERCISE 5.4

grammatical focus: participial phrases

mechanical focus: commas with participial phrases

When two events are described in the same sentence *and the subject of both sentences is the same,* it is possible to omit the first subject and use a participial phrase. Notice the following example.

After *many guests* rushed for the stairwell, *they* found it blocked.
After rushing for the stairwell, *many guests* found it blocked.

Notice that it is necessary to replace *they* with *many guests* in the main clause. Also, the comma after stairwell is still necessary.

In the following sentence, the first verb is in the past perfect tense. Notice the possible revision.

After many guests had broken their windows, they were faced with billowing smoke.
After having broken their windows, many guests were faced with billowing smoke.

The important thing to remember in using participial phrases is that the subject in both sentences must refer to the same person or object.

The following sentences describe additional events of the fire in the Las Vegas hotel. Wherever possible change the adverbial clause to a participial phrase. Remember this change is possible only if the subject in both clauses refers to the same person or thing.

1. While Mr. and Mrs. Terran were resting in their room on the 22nd floor, they heard the commotion in the hall.
2. After the 200 guests had elbowed their way to the exit, they found it filled with smoke.
3. While one guest was looking frantically for an exit, his wife collapsed.
4. After Mr. Casby noticed the smoke, he ran upstairs to rescue his parents.
5. While some guests were running out of the hotel with cash drawers in their hands, many dealers were rushing out stuffing chips in their pockets.

6. While Ann Westborough was trying to shinny down a rope, she lost her grip and fell.

7. While David Morgan was clambering down a fire ladder, he noticed that he was bleeding.

EXERCISE 5.5

rhetorical focus: action verbs

In order for a reader to understand exactly what happened during an event, it is important to describe the actions of the event carefully. Using verbs that precisely describe an action is one way to do this. Exercise 5.2 describes two accidents that Charles McLaughlin was involved in. Notice the verbs that are used to describe the accidents. In the first accident he *ran into* the roll-up door. In the second accident he *knocked down* the mailbox. In both sentences the writer could have merely stated that Mr. McLaughlin *drove into* the door or the mailbox. However, the two verbs that are used provide a more precise description of what occurred.

The sentences in Exercise 5.3 describe several things that many of the hotel guests did when the fire occurred. List three of these actions.

1.

2.

3.

Exercise 5.4 describes what some of the individual guests did during the fire:

Ann Westborough *shinnied* down a rope.
David Morgan *clambered* down a fire ladder.

In both sentences, it is possible to use *climbed*. However, the two verbs that are used more precisely described what happened. Write the dictionary definition of these two verbs:

- *shinny:*

- *clamber:*

The following verbs all describe different ways that a person can walk or move. For each verb, indicate when a person might move like this. For example, *to march* is to walk with measured steps at a steady rate. A person in a parade could walk like this.

	person who might
verb	**move like this**

1. *bustle:* to walk in a hurried or energetic manner

2. *creep:* to move on hands and knees with the body close to the ground

3. *dart:* to move suddenly and swiftly

4. *elbow:* to push or shove as with the elbows

5. *flounder:* to move clumsily as to regain balance

6. *hobble:* to move awkwardly or with difficulty

7. *limp:* to walk lamely with irregularity as if favoring one leg

8. *pace:* to walk back and forth

9. *plod:* to walk with great effort

10. *scramble:* to move or climb hurriedly, especially on the hands and knees

11. *scurry:* to move with light running steps

12. *shuffle:* to walk dragging the feet along the ground

13. *stalk:* to walk with a stiff and angry gait

14. *stroll:* to walk at a leisurely pace

15. *strut:* to walk proudly or pompously

16. *totter:* to walk unsteadily or feebly as if about to fall

EXERCISE 5.6

rhetorical focus: point of view

Sometimes it is important to describe an event objectively and not include your own feelings and attitudes. News reports and personnel files generally try to describe events objectively. Notice the difference in the following sentences.

1. One guest in the hotel lost her grip and fell while trying to shinny down a rope.
2. *Unfortunately,* one guest in the hotel lost her grip and fell while trying to shinny down a rope.
3. *One tragic consequence of the fire was that* one guest in the hotel lost her grip and fell while trying to shinny down a rope.

The italicized phrases in sentences two and three express the author's attitude toward the event. Notice that even one word can express an author's attitude.

The following passage describes the accidents of Charles McLaughlin. Compare this account with the accounts in Exercises 5.1 and 5.2. Then circle all the phrases that show the writer's attitude toward the incidents.

On March 13, while on duty, Charles McLaughlin, a very careless driver employed by Loomis armored cars, was involved in another accident. The accident occurred in Riverside, California. Not paying attention to his driving, Mr. McLaughlin turned right on Main and 33rd and collided with a Volkswagen Rabbit. This caused minor damage to the truck and serious damage to the car. On the basis of the police report, the Loomis accident committee correctly determined that Mr. McLaughlin had been quite careless. As a result of the committee's conclusion, the branch manager reported that he had talked with Mr. McLaughlin about his extremely poor driving record.

Further evidence of Mr. McLaughlin's irresponsibility occurred on May 6, when Mr. McLaughlin was returning from his shift. That day he ran into a roll-up door at the Loomis facility in Vallejo, causing significant damage to the door. Damage to the truck, however, was minor. Finally, on June 7, Mr. McLaughlin once again demonstrated his recklessness by knocking down several mailboxes near the edge of the company parking lot. There was damage to the mailboxes and minor damage to the truck.

The branch manager, David Rossi, stated that he had spoken with Mr. McLaughlin on several occasions about his driving record. Mr. Rossi added that he had warned Mr. McLaughlin that three preventable accidents in one year could lead to his discharge, as indeed it should.

Reading Selection

The Laws of Inheritance and Variation

One scientist who kept wondering about variations was a Dutch botanist, Hugo De Vries. In 1886, while he was taking a relaxing walk in the evening, he passed an empty lot in which evening primroses were growing. These were American flowers which had been introduced into the Netherlands not long before.

De Vries' botanical eye was caught by the evening primroses at once because some seemed quite different from others. They were all growing in a clump as though all had originated from the seeds of a single plant. If that were so, why shouldn't all the plants look alike and resemble their ancestor, whatever that ancestor looked like? Why should some be so different from others?

He began at once to study the flowers. He crossed one plant with the other and collected the seeds that resulted. He carefully noted the characteristics of the two parent plants. Then he studied the characteristics of the offspring plants that developed from the seeds.

These were the same sort of experiments that Mendel had done, and over a number of years de Vries worked out the same laws of inheritance that Mendel had worked out many years before.

EXERCISE 5.7

1. Underline the two verbs in paragraph 1 that are in the past progressive tense. Notice that this sentence describes three events in the past. What are they?

1.

2.

3.

Circle the action verb that could replace *was taking a relaxing walk.*

shuffle   stroll   stalk

Rewrite the following sentence using a participial phrase. Use the action verb.

While De Vries was taking a relaxing walk in the evening, he passed an empty lot.

2. In the second paragraph, circle the verb in the past perfect tense. What two events are described in this sentence? What is the problem that De Vries wished to study?
3. Paragraph 3 describes the experiment that De Vries did to study the problem. List the steps that he followed.

1.

2.

3.

4.

Notice that this paragraph describes a process. However, unlike the experiment in Chapter 1, this paragraph does not use the verb in the imperative. Rather the paragraph uses the past tense to describe an event that has already occurred. Rewrite the four steps as if you were telling someone how to study plant variation.

1.

2.

3.

4.

4. Circle the two verbs in paragraph 4 that are in the past perfect tense. Notice that the verb *work out* appears twice. Why is *worked out* used in one case and *had worked out* used in the other?

Writing Tasks

☐ SITUATION ONE
The Science Student

You are a science student. Your teacher has asked you to undertake two simple experiments to illustrate two principles of evaporation. You must then write up the experiment and your conclusions regarding the principles of evaporation.

☐ *TASK*

First follow the direction for the experiment listed below:

Find a saucer, a water glass, and a test tube. Put two tablespoons of water in each of them. Place them side by side and let them stand. From which one does the water evaporate first? Second? Why do you think this is so? What principle of evaporation does this demonstrate?

Now complete the following paragraph. Be sure to keep the verbs in the past tense and to use sentence connectors such as *first, next, finally.*

In order to study the speed of evaporation I undertook the following experiment. First, I....
    I discovered that....
    This experiment demonstrates that....

Now follow the directions for the second experiment. Write a second paragraph which describes what you did and what principle of evaporation was demonstrated.

Draw two squares of chalk of equal size on the blackboard. Rub each of them with a wet cloth. Now fan one of them. Which dries first? What principle of evaporation does this illustrate?

SITUATION TWO
The Supervisor

You are a supervisor in a Ford assembly plant. One of your employees has been accused of stealing. You need to write up the incident for his personnel file.

☐ TASK

Study the facts listed below about your employee, Bob Clark. Then write a paragraph in which you summarize the facts. Be sure to use the past, past perfect, or past progressive tense. Combine short sentences by using adverbial clauses or participial phrases.

facts:

- On September 20 Bob Clark leaves the plant.
- That day there is a check of lunch boxes.
- The supervisor finds a drill that belongs to the company in Bob Clark's lunch box.
- Bob Clark denies that he put the drill in his lunch box.
- On October 1 Bob Clark's co-worker notices Mr. Clark putting a screwdriver that belongs to the company in his pocket.
- Bob Clark says he is going to use it in the plant.
- On October 2 the supervisor discusses these two incidents with Bob Clark.
- The supervisor warns Bob Clark that thefts are grounds for disciplinary action.

SITUATION THREE
The Biologist

You are a biologist. You are writing an article on endangered species. You want to include one paragraph on the whooping crane, a bird that is rapidly disappearing in the United States.

☐ TASK ONE

Use the information below to write one paragraph which describes events that have affected the survival of the whooping crane. Begin by putting the events in order of time. Then write a paragraph in which you objectively describe these events.

_____However, man-made barriers managed to save the whooping crane from

the danger of oil.

_____By 1900 fewer than 100 birds were left.

_____During the 1970's the whooping crane faced great potential danger from oil spills.

_____From 1850–1900 the expansion of farmland produced a decrease in the natural habitats of the whooping crane.

_____One of those preserves was Aransas National Wildlife Refuge in Texas, which is a favorite winter home for the whooping cranes.

_____In the 1930's the United States government began to acquire land for wildlife preserves.

_____The oil slick reached the Texas coast near the Aransas National Wildlife refuge.

_____Although in 1938 the number of whooping cranes was down to 29, because of the preserves it was up to 74 by the 1970's.

_____In 1976, for example, a Mexican oil well off the Yucatan Peninsula developed a leak.

☐ *TASK TWO*

Now write a paragraph using the same information but including your attitude toward the decrease of the whooping crane population and the dangers presented by oil spills.

☐ SITUATION FOUR
The Reporter

You are a reporter for the *Sun Herald*. You write a weekly column in which you interview the person on the street about a personal question. This week your question is: What is the most dangerous (or exciting) thing you have ever done? (Select either *dangerous* or *exciting*.)

(The correct order is 9, 2, 6, 1, 4, 3, 8, 5, 7)

□ TASK

Interview two people. Ask them to describe the most dangerous (or exciting) thing they have ever done. Select one of the interviews and write a brief paragraph in which you summarize what they said. Use the first person and keep the verbs in the past tense. (For example, if Ed Duncan were one of the people you interviewed you would write: Ed Duncan: The most dangerous experience I ever had was when I was a child. . . .) Try to use action verbs in your description.

□ SITUATION FIVE
The Creative Writing Student

You are a student in a creative writing class. Your teacher has asked you to observe an event and note the actions of the people. You are supposed to give special attention to the way the people move and what this says about them.

□ TASK

Attend an event. It can be a personal event such as a wedding, a cultural event such as a symphony, or a public event such as a city meeting. Observe the way in which various people enter and leave the event. Then write a short paper in which you describe this event. Focus on the people you observed. Describe the manner in which they walked and what you concluded about the kind of person they were. You may find the verbs in Exercise 5.5 helpful.

Peer Correction of Student Compositions

The Reporter

(1) This week the interview question is: What is the most dangerous thing you have ever done?

(2) Mr. Nelson Toreno: The most dangerous experience I ever had was on July 1967. (3) I was in Caracas and it is about 7 o'clock when suddenly the earth begin to shake. (4) On the beginning I didn't realized it was an earthquake, but then my brothers and mother started to shouted, "Earthquake! Earthquake!"

(5) Ranning from the house I heard a voice coming from inside. (6) Mother said, "It's Fernando; something happen to him." (7) I ran into the house and looked for him.

(8) He lock himself in the bathroom. (9) We pushed down the door and ran out again.

(10) Not known what to do, we decided to go see our father, who was out of the city. (11) Two blocks from the city I heard people crying and saw buildings that fell down. (12) I thank God we were all alive.

practice in correcting

The composition above has several errors in it. Follow the instructions below and correct the composition as directed.

Sentence 2: Correct the error in the choice of preposition.

Sentence 3: Correct the errors in verb tense.

Sentence 4: Correct the error in the choice of preposition. Correct the errors in verb form.

Sentence 5: Correct the error in the participle. Supply the missing punctuation.

Sentence 6: Correct the error in verb tense.

Sentence 8: Correct the error in verb tense; use the past perfect tense.

Sentence 10: Use the correct form of the participle.

Sentence 11: Correct the error in verb tense; use the past perfect tense.

Sentence 12: Correct the error in verb tense.

II

DEFINING

6. Defining by Example

7. Defining by Classification

8. Defining by Comparison and Contrast

6

Defining
by Example

Several techniques can be used to define a term. If a term refers to a concrete object, such as a chair, you could use any one of three techniques. First, you could point to a concrete example of a chair. Second, you could describe the typical size and shape of a chair and the material from which it is made. Finally, you could describe the purpose of the chair. All of these techniques are ways of defining a chair. Generally, of course, it is not important who made the chair or who uses the chair. What is important is the material it is made of and its function. Thus, the definition should be written to emphasize these elements. If a term is an abstraction, such as angular distance or a holiday, one effective method of defining the term is to point to a specific example of the abstraction. This chapter is devoted to defining concrete and abstract terms by using examples.

EXERCISE 6.1

grammatical focus: passive voice

Since in defining a concrete object it is the material and function of the object that are important, the passive voice is frequently used. Notice the following example.

A manufacturing company makes a chair of wood, foam, or leather.
A chair is made of wood, foam, or leather (by a manufacturing company).

The passive voice is formed by putting the object *(chair)* in the subject position and adding a form of the verb *to be (is)* with the past participle of the verb *(made)*. The subject *(a manufacturing company)* is introduced by the preposition *by*. It can be either included or deleted. In this case, since it is not important who performed the action, it would be best to delete it.

The following sentences describe the construction material and purpose of the carpenter tools introduced in Chapter 2. In order to emphasize the material and purpose of these objects, change the sentences to the passive voice. Omit the person who performed the action.

example:

An individual uses a chair to sit on.
A chair is used to sit on.

1. A manufacturing company makes a miter box of wood or cast iron.
2. A carpenter uses a miter box to guide a saw to cut 45° angles and accurate squared ends.
3. A manufacturing company makes a windup tape measure of steel or linen.
4. A carpenter uses a windup tape measure to measure large areas.
5. A manufacturing company makes a round knife of steel and wood.
6. A carpenter uses a round knife to cut leather.
7. A manufacturing company makes a plasterer's trowel of steel and wood.
8. A carpenter uses a plasterer's trowel to apply and smooth plaster.

EXERCISE 6.2

grammatical focus: passive voice

The following items are commonly found in a chemistry lab. For each object write one sentence to describe what it is made of and how it is used. Be sure to use the passive voice. For example:

object	material	function
flask	glass	to hold liquids

A flask is made of glass and is used to hold liquids.

object	material	function
1. funnel	glass	to channel liquid into a flask
2. centrifuge	metal	to separate materials of different densities
3. test tube holder	wood	to store test tubes
4. Bunsen burner	metal	to produce very hot flames
5. litmus paper	paper dipped in litmus	to test for acids and bases

Describe the construction material and function of at least three other items typically found in a chemistry lab such as a stirring rod, beaker, or test tube.

1.

2.

3.

EXERCISE 6.3

grammatical focus: appositives

mechanical focus: commas with appositives

A sentence that defines the construction material and purpose of litmus paper will be adequate only if a person knows what litmus is. In order to write a complete definition of litmus paper, it might be important to add the following information.

Litmus paper is a purple coloring matter obtained from various lichens.

We could then have two sentences to define litmus.

Litmus paper is made from purple paper dipped in litmus.
Litmus is purple coloring matter obtained from various lichens.

However, since both sentences contain the word litmus, the sentences could be combined as follows.

Litmus paper is made from paper dipped in litmus, which is a purple coloring matter obtained from various lichens.

OR

Litmus paper is made from paper dipped in litmus, a purple coloring matter obtained from various lichens.

Notice the use of commas in both examples. The second sentence, in which the words *which is* have been deleted, is called an *appositive*. An appositive must be set off from the rest of the sentence by commas.

The following chart defines the four basic components of a computer. Write a sentence that combines this information by using an appositive. Be sure to add the necessary articles. For example:

term	definition	function
Litmus	a purple coloring matter obtained from various lichens	used in litmus paper to test for acids and bases

Litmus, a purple coloring matter obtained from various lichens, is used in litmus paper to test for acids and bases.

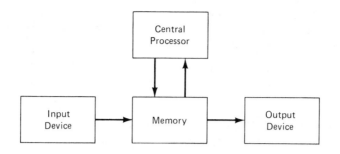

term	definition	function
1. computer memory	an ordered sequence of storage locations	to store information
2. central processor	the control unit of the computer	to coordinate all the operation of the computer
3. input device	frequently a computer terminal	to enter data into the computer memory
4. output device	frequently a computer terminal	to display results in a readable form

(Adapted from Elliot Koffman and Frank L. Friedman. *Problem Solving and Structured Programming in Basic Reading.* Reading, Mass.: Addison-Wesley Publishing, 1979, p. 3.)

EXERCISE 6.4

grammatical focus: appositives

The following chart describes three major holidays in the United States. Combine the information on each into one sentence by using an appositive.

holiday	date	purpose
1. Thanksgiving	held on the fourth Thursday in November	commemorates the landing of the Pilgrims at Plymouth Rock
2. Christmas	held on December 25	celebrates the birth of Christ
3. New Year's Day	held on January 1	celebrates a new year

If the function of these sentences is to emphasize the purpose of the holiday, then it is best to write the sentence with this information in the main clause as you have done.

Halloween, held on October 31, *commemorates the night before All Saints' Day.*

If, however, it is important to emphasize the date of a holiday, it would be better to include this information in the main clause.

Halloween, a commemoration of the night before All Saints' Day, *is held on October 31.*

Imagine that you are writing a paragraph that describes when several major holidays in the United States are celebrated. Rewrite the three sentences describing Thanksgiving, Christmas, and New Year's Day so that the sentences emphasize the date.

1. Thanksgiving

2. Christmas

3. New Year's Day

Write three sentences in which you describe the date and purpose of major holidays in your country. Write them so that you emphasize the purpose of these holidays.

1.

2.

3.

EXERCISE 6.5

rhetorical focus: parallel structure with infinitives and gerunds

rhetorical focus: sentence connectors of exemplification

Abstractions such as honesty must be defined with different techniques than those used with objects. Either of the following techniques can be used to define an abstraction. First, you could describe the typical behavior of someone who has this quality.

For example, an honest person is someone who always tells the truth.

Second, you could indicate what effect this behavior has on other people.

For example, an honest person is usually trusted by other people.

Suppose you want to define the term *to plod*. You can, of course, use a definition such as the following.

To plod is to walk with a great deal of effort.

Notice that since the infinitive *to plod* is used, the infinitive *to walk* is used. It is also possible to use the noun form, *plodding*. This is called a *gerund*. If *plodding* is used, then the gerund *walking* should also be used.

Plodding is walking with a great deal of effort.

This sentence provides the reader with a formal definition of *to plod*. However, to provide a more complete definition, a specific example of the typical behavior of a person who is plodding could be given.

Plodding is walking with a great deal of effort. For example, when I go to the mountains in January, I always plod through the snow.

Since the second sentence is a specific example of plodding, the sentence could be introduced by any of the following terms.

For example,	As an illustration,
For instance,	As an example,
To give an example,	To illustrate,

Notice that these terms are followed by a comma.

Write a formal definition for ten of the terms listed on the next page. Be sure to use parallel structure by using an infinitive with an infinitive and a gerund with a gerund. Then add a sentence that exemplifies this type of behavior. You can use either your own or someone else's behavior. Introduce this sentence with an introductory phrase such as *for example, as an example, to illustrate.*

example

To stroll is to walk leisurely. For instance, I generally stroll through the park on Sunday afternoons.

1. to plod	9. to wish
2. to saunter	10. to crave
3. to chuckle	11. to acquire
4. to laugh	12. to earn
5. to daydream	13. to watch
6. to meditate	14. to stare
7. to ask	15. to listen
8. to beg	16. to hear

Reading Selection

Angular Distance

Angular distance is a term used to describe the size of the angle an object moves through in a given time. For example, a nearby plane, moving at the very same speed as a distant one, covers a greater angular distance than the distant

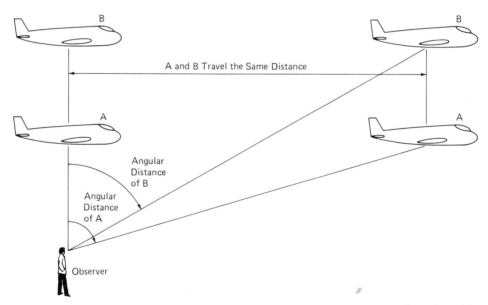

one. As we would expect, the same is true of the stars. The more distant ones appear to take a longer time to shift their positions one degree of distance than do stars that are nearby. A typical nearby star takes about 10,000 years to shift its position one degree. A typical distant star, on the other hand, takes about 100,000 years to move one degree.

EXERCISE 6.6

1. In this passage, what term is being defined?
2. What is the formal definition that is given for this term?
3. What example is given to help define the term?
   Circle the expression that is used to introduce the illustration.
4. What fact about stars does the example help to explain?

Reading Selection

Social Gestures

Among the kinds of social gestures most significant for second-language teachers are those which are the same in form but different in meaning in the two cultures. These might be called the ambiguous gestures. For example, a Colombian who wants someone to approach him often signals with a hand movement in which all the fingers of one hand, cupped, point downward as they move rapidly back and forth. Speakers of English have a similar gesture (though the hand may not be cupped and the fingers may be held more loosely) but for them the gesture means *goodbye* or *go away*, quite the opposite of the Colombian gesture. Again, in Colombia, a speaker of English would have to know that when he indicates height he must choose between different gestures depending on whether he is referring to a human being or an animal. If he keeps the palm of the hand parallel to the floor, as he would in his own culture when indicating the height of a child, for example, he will very likely be greeted by laughter; in Colombia this gesture is reserved for the description of animals. In order to describe human beings he should keep the palm of his hand at right angles to the floor. Substitutions of one gesture for the other often create not only humorous but embarrassing moments. In both of the examples above, speakers from two different cultures have the same gesture, physically, but its meaning differs sharply.

(Source: "Gestures in the Language Classroom" from *Readings on English as a Second Language* by Kenneth Croft. Copyright © 1972, 1980. Reprinted by permission of Winthrop Publishers, Inc., Cambridge, Massachusetts.)

EXERCISE 6.7

1. What term is being defined in this paragraph? Underline the sentence that lists the term that is being defined. Is the verb in the active or passive voice? Write your own definition of this term.

2. What two examples are given to help define the term?
   Circle all the phrases that are used to introduce the examples.

Writing Tasks

SITUATION ONE
The Chemistry Student

You are a chemistry student. You have just completed a simple experiment to test for acids and bases. You have written up the experiment as follows.

First, I used blue litmus paper to test for acids. I gathered a small amount of vinegar, water, lemon juice, sweet milk, and liquid soap. I placed the end of five pieces of litmus paper into each of the liquids. Whereas the vinegar and lemon juice caused the paper to turn pink, the other substances caused no change.

Next, I used pink litmus paper to test for bases. I placed pink litmus paper into each of the liquids. Whereas the liquid soap caused the paper to turn blue, the other substances had no effect on the paper. Thus, I concluded that vinegar and lemon juice are examples of acids while liquid soap is an example of a base.

To emphasize the results of the experiment rather than the fact that you completed it, you have decided to rewrite the passage in the passive voice.

☐ TASK

Rewrite the active sentences in the passive voice. The first sentence is done for you. Be sure to keep the verb in the passive voice and to omit the agent *(by me)*. Check that the verb agrees in number with the subject. (Notice that the sentence beginning with "I concluded that . . ." must be revised to "It was concluded that . . .")

First, blue litmus paper was used to test for acids.

SITUATION TWO
The Computer Programmer

You are a computer programmer. You are writing a manual on BASIC programming. You have decided to start with a definition of programming in general,
followed by a definition of BASIC.

☐ TASK

Write the first two paragraphs of the manual. In the first paragraph include
the following information.

1. A formal definition of programming, which is the act of designing a list of instructions
   for the computer. These instructions must be exact and in a certain order.
2. An example of how writing a computer program is like describing how to assemble
   a bicycle. Each step must be done correctly and in the right order or the bicycle will
   not work properly.

Use the paragraph on angular distance as a model for the first paragraph.

In the second paragraph include the following information on BASIC. Use
the passive voice to place BASIC in the subject position and try to combine
information by using appositives.

1. BASIC is an abbreviation of *Beginner's All-Purpose Symbolic Instruction Code.*
2. Dartmouth College developed BASIC programming language.
3. Most computers cannot execute BASIC programming directly.
4. Computers must translate BASIC programs into language that is understood by the
   computer.

SITUATION THREE
The International Student

You are an international student. Your English teacher has asked you to write
a brief description of three major holidays in your country. She has asked that
for each holiday you include the date and purpose of the holiday, along with
one or two examples of the typical ways the holiday is celebrated.

☐ TASK

Write the paragraph on holidays in your country. Use Exercise 6.4 as a
model for using appositives to combine the date and purpose of the holiday

in one sentence. Introduce the examples of how the holiday is celebrated with sentence connectors of exemplification.

SITUATION FOUR
The Communication Student

You are a student in a communication class. Currently your class is studying how people communicate through gestures, particularly by the way they walk. Your teacher has asked you to select four types of walking and provide examples of when you have observed this type of walking. You have selected the four types of walking pictured on the next page.

☐ *TASK*

Begin by writing a sentence definition for each of these types of walking, along with an example. Use parallel structure in your definition and introduce the example with a sentence connector of exemplification. For instance, for *strolling*, you might write the following.

> To stroll is to walk leisurely. Strolling often indicates that a person has plenty of time and no special purpose. For example, last Sunday, I noticed many people strolling around the new shops in the Renaissance Plaza.

Then write a paragraph in which you define the four types of walking and provide examples of when and where you have observed this type of walking. Be sure to start the paragraph with a general statement of how walking is one important type of nonverbal communication.

Definition: To pace is to

or

Pacing is

Example:

Definition: To scurry is to

or

Scurrying is

Example:

Definition: To strut is to

or

Strutting is

Example:

UNEMPLOYMENT OFFICE ➡

Definition: To shuffle is to

or

Shuffling is

Example:

Peer Correction of Student Compositions

The International Student

(1) Although there are twelve legal holidays in Japan, all of them are not the major holidays. (2) I chose three holidays to describe which are related to age, namely, Adult's Day, Children's Day, and Respect for the Aged Day.

(3) First, Adult's Day which is celebrate on January 15 is for people who are conscious of being adults and who try to live for themselves. (4) People hold ceremonies at every City Hall. (5) Most of men wear the business suits, and about two thirds of women wear "furisodes," beautiful and gorgeous kimonos.

(6) Second, Children's Day, celebrated on May 5, is for children and has many festivities. (7) For example most families make or buy the carp streamers, which is made of paper or cloth, and fly them out of the windows.

(8) Third, Respect for the Aged Day, celebrated on September 15, shows respect for the old. (9) Many parties is celebrated on this new holiday which began in 1952.

practice in correcting

The composition above has several errors in it. Follow the instructions below and correct the composition as directed.

Sentence 1: Correct the error in the use of articles.
Sentence 3: Correct the error in the verb in the passive voice. Add the necessary punctuation.
Sentence 4: Change the sentence to the passive voice.
Sentence 5: Correct the errors in the use of the articles.
Sentence 7: Add the necessary punctuation. Correct the errors in the use of articles. Correct the errors in subject–verb agreement.
Sentence 9: Correct the error in subject–verb agreement.

7

Defining by Classification

At times the best way to define a very general term such as *learning* is to distinguish various types of learning. For instance, learning might be divided into formal learning, which takes place in a classroom, and informal learning, which takes place outside a classroom. Sometimes the categories are very rigidly distinguished by agreed-upon standards. In biology, for example, an animal is classified as a reptile or an amphibian according to a set of agreed-upon characteristics. At other times, however, a classification is based upon individual perception. For instance, a sociologist might classify types of societies; while his or her classification might be shared by other scholars, undoubtedly there will be other ways of viewing societies.

EXERCISE 7.1

grammatical focus: verb tense: present perfect

A common technique for starting a paper that discusses a general topic such as learning or culture is to describe how various scholars have defined the term. Many times the present perfect tense is used for this definition. Even though this tense describes something that occurred in the past, the use of the present perfect suggests that the action still has significance for the present. It is quite appropriate to write, "Alvin Toffler *distinguished* two types of future shock." However, if the present perfect is used ("Alvin Toffler *has distinguished* two types of future shock"), it suggests that the writer of the paper intends to examine or elaborate on Toffler's classification. The present perfect tense is formed by using the present tense of *to have* and the past particle of the main verb.

    Use the following information to write a sentence using the present perfect tense. For example:

scholar	verb of clas-sification	classification
Alvin Toffler	distinguish	two types of future shock

Alvin Toffler has distinguished two types of future shock.

scholar	verb of clas-sification	classification
1. Marshall McLuhan	classify	media according to two dimensions
2. Milton Gordon	discuss	two types of cul-tural traits
3. Carl Rogers	categorize	learning into two modes
4. Edward T. Hall	define	three kinds of time
5. Eric Berne	delineate	three ego states

Write two additional sentences which describe someone's classification of a concept.

6.

7.

EXERCISE 7.2

grammatical focus: review of nonrestrictive relative clauses

mechanical focus: colons introducing categories

Readers, of course, want more information than just the fact that Alvin Toffler distinguished two types of future shock. They want to know what these categories are. Colons are often used to provide this additional information, as in the following example.

Alvin Toffler has distinguished two types of future shock: physical shock and psychological shock.

This, however, will generally still not satisfy readers. They also wish to know what is meant by the categories. This information can be added by using relative clauses as in the following example.

Alvin Toffler has distinguished two types of future shock: physical shock, which includes such things as adapting to new environments and illnesses; and psychological shock, which includes such things as adjusting to new inventions and discoveries.

Notice that since the sentence contains two nonrestrictive relative clauses, the comma after the first clause ("which includes such things as adapting to new environments and illnesses") has been replaced with a semicolon.

Add the following information to the sentences in Exercise 7.1 by using a colon and relative clauses. Then indicate into which category the listed item belongs.

scholar	categories	description of categories
1. Marshall McLuhan	hot media	require little participation, like the radio
	cool media	require a great deal of participation, like the telephone

According to McLuhan's categories, where would you place a lecture? A small group discussion?

2. Milton Gordon	intrinsic traits	include religion, beliefs, and literature
	extrinsic traits	include dress and speech patterns

According to Gordon's categories, where would you place a poem? A business suit? A dialect?

3. Carl Rogers	rote learning	involves the mind only
	experiential learning	involves the whole person

According to Roger's categories, where would you place memorizing vocabulary items? Learning a sport? Solving a math problem?

4. Edward T. Hall	formal time	is known by everyone and taken for granted
	informal time	is imprecise time like "later" and "in a minute"
	technical time	is used by scientists

According to Hall's categories, where would you put the following expressions? "Just a second" "Two o'clock" "12 minutes and 13.006 seconds"

5. Eric Berne	Parent	comes from parental figures
	Adult	makes decisions on an objective basis
	Child	responds the way a child would

According to Berne's categories, which ego state is expressed in the following sentences?

"You should say you're sorry."
"I don't want to say I'm sorry."
"Why do I need to apologize?"

Add a description of the categories you wrote in Exercise 7.1.

6.

7.

EXERCISE 7.3

grammatical focus: review of the passive voice

At times the classification of a concept is generally agreed upon by scholars in the field. For example, astronomers generally classify the nine planets according to the inner and outer planets. In the previous exercises it was important to know who designed the classification since there were many other ways of dividing the topic. In the case of the classification of the planets, however, what is important is the categories rather than the person who designed them. Thus, it is more appropriate to use the passive voice ("The nine planets are divided into inner and outer planets") than the active voice ("Astronomers divide the nine planets into inner and outer planets").

Use the categories and verbs of classification listed below to write a sentence in the passive voice. Notice that it is possible to use the modals *can* or *may* with the verb *to be*. For example:

categories	verb of classification
planets:	are divided into
inner and outer planets	

The planets are divided into inner and outer planets.

	categories	verb of classification
1.	ships:	
	passenger and cargo ships	can be classified according to
2.	chemical substances:	
	compounds and mixtures	are categorized as
3.	books:	
	hardback and paperback books	are divided into
4.	trees:	
	deciduous and nondeciduous trees	can be classified as
5.	sounds:	
	voiced and voiceless sounds	can be categorized as
6.	strikes:	
	economic strikes, sympathy strikes, and safety strikes	may be divided into
7.	language tests:	
	achievement, aptitude, and proficiency tests	can be classified as

Write two additional sentences in the passive voice in which you describe a system of classification.

8.

9.

EXERCISE 7.4

rhetorical focus: sentence connectors of classification

Of course, readers want more information than just the names of categories. They want to know what these categories mean. One technique is to add a relative clause to the sentence as was done in the previous exercise. However, if the explanation is rather long, a full sentence can be used to explain each item. These sentences can begin with the name of the category or with one of the following expressions.

- The former / The latter (used when there are only two categories)
- The first / First

- The second / Second
- The last / Last

Use the information provided below to write additional sentences that explain the items introduced in Exercise 7.3. Use one of the expressions listed above.

example

- Planets:
  Inner—includes Mercury, Venus, Earth, Mars
  Outer—includes Jupiter, Saturn, Uranus, Neptune

The nine planets are divided into inner and outer planets. The inner planets include Mercury, Venus, Earth, and Mars. The outer planets include Jupiter, Saturn, Uranus, and Neptune.
>   OR
The nine planets are divided into inner and outer planets. The former include Mercury, Venus, Earth, and Mars. The latter include Jupiter, Saturn, Uranus, and Neptune.

1. Ships:
   passenger ships—used primarily to transport passengers
   cargo ships—used primarily to transport freight

2. Chemical substances:
   compounds—composed of substances that have lost their identity
   mixtures—composed of substances that have kept their identity

3. Books:
   hardbook—bound in cloth, cardboard, or leather
   paperback—bound in paper

4. Trees:
   deciduous—sheds all of its leaves each year
   nondeciduous—does not shed its leaves

5. Sounds:
   voiced—produced with the vocal chords vibrating
   voiceless—produced with the vocal chords apart

6. Strikes:
   economic—is a strike for higher wages, better fringe benefits, or better working conditions
   sympathy—is a strike to honor the picket lines of another union
   safety—is a strike to protest existing working conditions

7. Language tests:
   achievement test—measures how well a person has mastered a specific part of the language
   aptitude test—measures a person's ability to learn a language
   proficiency test—measures how well a person knows the language

Add descriptive sentences for each of the categories you listed in Exercise 7.3.

8.

9.

EXERCISE 7.5

rhetorical focus: dividing a topic

The most important step in classifying is to design categories that will include all of the items that need to be classified. Furthermore, the categories should be carefully chosen so that each item will fit in only one category. For instance, a biologist wants to have enough categories so that all plant life can be classified. However, the classification system will not be valuable if one plant can fit in three classes. Often there are several ways to classify items. Transportation, for example, could be classified by the speed of transportation, by the cost, or by the mode (by land, by sea, or by air).
   Supply possible categories for the listed items below. As you will notice, one item can be divided in several ways. For example:

item	system of classification	categories
books	by type of binding	hardback
		paperback

item	system of classification	categories
1. books	by content	
2. books	by author	
3. movies	by length	
4. movies	by audience appeal	
5. restaurants	by the type of food served	

item	system of classification	categories
6. restaurants	by the service provided	
7. universities	by the degrees offered	
8. universities	by the source of funding	
9. students	by their place of residence	
10. students	by their grade point average	
11. classes	by the content of the course	
12. classes	by the course requirements	
13. teachers	by their experience	
14. teachers	by their rank	
15. jobs	by the type of work	
16. jobs	by the salary and benefits	

EXERCISE 7.6

rhetorical focus: categorizing data

Once a topic has been divided on some basis, the criteria for placing an item into each group need to be defined. For example, if you categorized transportation by cost as expensive and inexpensive, you would need to indicate what is meant by these terms. One possibility would be to determine how much it costs to travel ten miles by different methods of transportation and then to select a point at which, according to your definition, you would classify the cost as expensive.

Biologists in classifying plant and animal life have specific criteria for determining in which class an item belongs. The exercise below describes several classifications used by biologists. Following each description there is a list of specific items that can fit in one or the other category. For each group begin by carefully reading the definition for each class and then decide into which group each item belongs.

example:

- annual—a plant with a short life cycle of one season
- perennial—a plant that blooms each growing season without having to be replanted

item	class
1. tomato	annual
2. rose	perennial
3. lily	perennial
4. radish	annual
5. trees	perennial

- vertebrate—an animal that has a backbone or spinal column
- invertebrate—an animal without a backbone or spinal column

item	class
1. human being	
2. butterfly	
3. horse	
4. fish	
5. oyster	
6. spider	
7. cow	
8. deer	
9. clam	
10. monkey	

- autotroph—an organism capable of manufacturing its own food by synthesis of inorganic materials as in photosynthesis
- heterotroph—an organism that obtains nourishment from organic substances and cannot manufacture its own food

item	**class**
1. human being	
2. rose	
3. butterfly	
4. fish	
5. radish	
6. mold .	
7. deer	
8. lily	
9. bee	
10. tomato	

- mollusk—an invertebrate that generally lives in the water and has a shell
- arthropod—an invertebrate that has horny segmented external coverings such as an insect

item	**class**
1. butterfly	
2. clam	
3. wasp	
4. oyster	
5. fly	
6. scallop	
7. spider	
8. dragonfly	
9. bee	
10. snail	

EXERCISE 7.7

rhetorical focus: conciseness

To be concise is to express an idea in as few words as is necessary. The opposite of conciseness is redundancy, or using more words than is necessary. There are several types of redundancy. One type involves repeating the same idea in another way, as in the following sentence.

An intransitive verb can stand alone by itself.

Since *alone* and *by itself* mean the same thing, there is no need to include both expressions. Either of the following sentences is more concise.

An intransitive verb can stand alone.
>   OR
An intransitive verb can stand by itself.

Another type of redundancy is padding, or using words that add no further information, as in the following sentence.

An intransitive verb is a verb that can stand alone in a sentence.

It is understood that an intransitive verb is a verb and that verbs occur in sentences. Thus, there is no need to use the phrases, *is a verb that* and *in a sentence.*

In each of the following sentences cross out any words or phrases that merely repeat an idea or add no further information.

example

A transitive verb must have a direct object or a noun that follows the verb. ·

1. The San Francisco Bay Area is a special place compared to other places because of its heterogeneous population or many ethnic groups.
2. In the past few years I have gone to many restaurants in the Bay Area to have breakfast, lunch, or dinner.
3. Bay Area restaurants can be categorized according to type of food such as American food or ethnic food like Japanese, Italian, Mexican, French, or Middle Eastern.

4. Restaurants in the Bay Area can be divided into three price categories which depend on cost: expensive, medium, and inexpensive.

5. Before getting into the heart of this essay, I would like to first define the terms expensive, medium, and inexpensive.

6. Expensive means that a meal will cost over fifteen dollars for each person.

7. There are many expensive restaurants in the Bay Area which cost a lot of money.

8. At Jack's it is common and very typical to wait one hour for a table.

9. At Narsai's a customer can relax and wait for the waiter to bring the food that you ordered from him to your table.

10. At Tycoon's it is difficult and almost impossible to find a place to park your car.

Reading Selection

In the following selection, Edward Hall discusses the three categories that he and his colleague, George Trager, use to describe Americans' concept of time.

Americans' Concept of Time

The ease with which Americans tend to polarize their thoughts about events may make it difficult for them to embrace an approach which employs three categories rather than two. Yet that is what I would like to propose here: a theory which suggests that culture has three levels. I have termed these the formal, informal, and technical, familiar terms but with new and expanded meanings.

Trager and I arrived at this tripartite theory as a result of some rather detailed and lengthy observations as to the way in which Americans talk about and handle time. We discovered that there were three kinds of time: formal time, which everyone knows about and takes for granted and which is well worked into daily life; informal time, which has to do with situational or imprecise references like "awhile," "later," "in a minute," and so on; technical time, an entirely different system used by scientists and technicians, in which even the terminology may be unfamiliar to the non-specialist. Having observed how these time systems are used and learned, and knowing something of their history, we realized that in other areas of his life man also approaches activities as formal, informal, or technical. In other words, we discovered that man has not two but three modes of behavior. Our generalizations about time had much broader applications than we originally supposed.

(Source: Edward T. Hall. *The Silent Language.* Greenwich, Conn.: Fawcett Publications, Inc., 1959, p. 66.)

EXERCISE 7.8

1. In the first paragraph Hall uses the present perfect tense (*I* have *termed*) rather than the past tense (*I termed*). By doing so he suggests that he will proceed to elaborate on these terms.
   Since Hall is describing a classification system which he and his colleague Trager have devised, he uses the active rather than passive voice. Circle all the references that the author makes to himself in the selection (i.e., all the uses of *I* and *we*).

2. Listed below are several comments about time. For each item indicate if the comment represents a formal, informal, or technical view of time.

   a. "See you soon."

   b. "All officers must report for duty at 0700."

   c. "It's twelve o'clock."

   d. "The doctor will be with you shortly."

   e. "The class is scheduled for one hour and forty-five minutes."

   f. "The experiment measured the driver's reaction time to 1/100th of a second."

3. Punctuate the following sentence taken from the text. Then check the text to see if you have done it correctly.

   We discovered that there were three kinds of time formal time which everyone knows about and takes for granted and which is well worked into daily life informal time which has to do with situational or imprecise references like awhile later in a minute and so on technical time an entirely different system used by scientists and technicians in which even the terminology may be unfamiliar to the non-specialist.

Writing Tasks

SITUATION ONE
The Entertainment Guide Reviewer

You write a weekly column on dining out in the San Francisco Bay Area. This week you intend to describe the restaurants listed on the next page.

☐ TASK

First, decide on a way to arrange the restaurants such as by location, type of food, or expense. Then write the first paragraph of your review in which you indicate how you have grouped the restaurants and include examples for each category. Use a sentence in the passive voice to introduce your classification system. If you choose to categorize the restaurants by cost, be certain to indicate what is meant by each term.

restaurant	location	type of food	price
Casa de Eva	Berkeley	Mexican	inexpensive
Fugetsu	Berkeley	Japanese	medium
The Great American Restaurant	Oakland	American	medium
Lorenzo's	Oakland	American	expensive
La Mexicana	Oakland	Mexican	inexpensive
Jack's	San Francisco	American	expensive
Narsai's	Berkeley	French	expensive
North Beach Restaurant	San Francisco	Italian	expensive
Ota Fuku Tei	San Francisco	Japanese	inexpensive
Phoenician	Berkeley	Middle Eastern	inexpensive
Le Rhone	San Francisco	French	expensive
Tycoon	San Francisco	Middle Eastern	medium

☐ SITUATION TWO
The Grammar Student

You are a student in an English grammar class. Your teacher has given you a list of English sentences which exemplify the two types of verbs in English. He has asked you to study the examples and describe the two types of verbs.

☐ TASK

First, study the list of grammatical and ungrammatical sentences listed below. Then write a brief paragraph in which you describe the characteristics of transitive and intransitive verbs in English. Use the passive voice to describe the classification and provide several examples for each kind of verb. (Use examples other than the ones listed below.)

grammatical sentences	ungrammatical sentences
1. Andrew shops.	1. Andrew shops Ann.
2. The child cries.	2. The child cries Andrew.

grammatical sentences	ungrammatical sentences
3. Ann works.	3. Ann works Andrew.
4. Andrew likes Ann.	4. Andrew likes.
5. Ann disciplines the child.	5. Ann disciplines.
6. The child hugs Andrew.	6. The child hugs.

SITUATION THREE
The ESL Teacher

You are an ESL teacher. You teach a grammar class at a language institute. It is the end of the semester so you need to submit grades for your students. Three grades are possible: Pass, Fail, Pass with Distinction. The director of the school has asked that this semester you attach to your grades a brief paragraph in which you explain your standards for assigning students a Pass, Fail, or Pass with Distinction. For each student you have kept a record of the following information: their initial and final scores on the CELT (Comprehensive English Language Test for Speakers of English as a Second Language), their attendance, their scores on grammar quizzes, and their submission of homework assignments.

TASK

First, consider the following questions:

1. Which do you view as more important: a student's final score on the CELT or the progress the student makes from the first test to the final test?
2. How much emphasis will you place on attendance? Will there be a minimum attendance requirement for students to pass the course?
3. How important are the scores on the grammar quizzes?
4. How important is homework?

Second, on the basis of your answers to these questions, assign grades to each of the students listed below.

Finally, write a brief report to your director in which you explain on what basis you assigned students a Pass, Fail, or Pass with Distinction.

Be sure to attach your grade sheet to this report.

		CELT			
student	initial	final	absences	quizzes	homework
1. Arnoux, M.	53	83	0	10 18 12 21	√ √ − + √ √
2. Chang, Z.	72	79	1	18 15 16 19	− √ √ + √
3. Gao, Z.	69	69	4	12 17 19	√ √ − √
4. Irie, A.	72	89	0	19 21 25 22	+ + √ + √ +
5. Ishigamo, H.	64	84	7	15 13	√ √ √
6. Lee, M.	91	91	2	21 10 25 8	− √ − − + +
7. Nagahama, Y.	67	85	0	15 12 18 16	− √
8. Ristic, J.	64	67	1	21 25 24 22	√ + + + √ +
9. Sano, E.	85	89	6	22 21 19 21	
10. Zerpa, S.	69	92	0	19 15 24 25	+ + √ + √ √

Note: 100 points are possible on the CELT; 25 points are possible on the grammar quizzes. On the homework, + indicates good; √ indicates average; − indicates poor.

SITUATION FOUR
The Union Organizer

You are a union organizer. You have been asked to help the workers of Middlebrook Grocery Store form a union. The first thing you must do is to categorize the workers in the store according to a standard classification of grocery store employees. Then you can write a brief report which indicates into which category each employee of Middlebrook would fit under a standard food union contract.

☐ TASK

Begin by carefully reading the job description of each category of grocery store employee listed below. Then examine the list of employees at Middlebrook Grocery Store and decide into which category each employee would fit. Consider the present duties of each employee and use this to determine into which class he or she belongs. Finally, complete the report which is started below to give to the Middlebrook employees. Describe *in your own words* the duties of each category of grocery store employees and list the employees of Middlebrook who would fit into each category.

Classification of Grocery Store Employees

Managing Clerk: Every store shall have a managing clerk. A managing clerk is an employee who has general supervision over the employees of one store.

Senior Head Clerk: This classification shall apply to an employee who acts as assistant to the managing clerk or owner and is commonly known as the "second person" in the store.

Senior Produce Clerk: This classification shall apply to an employee who goes to the wholesale produce market to buy produce, or who is in charge of the produce section.

Head Clerk: The head clerk assists in the operation of the produce section. He conducts the operation of the store in the temporary absence of the managing clerk, the senior head clerk, or the owner, and is responsible for the opening and closing of the store. Finally, he has the authority and responsibility of buying and selecting merchandise for a department such as the frozen foods or dairy products.

Journeyman Clerk: A journeyman clerk is an employee who has gained 2,080 hours of experience in the retail food industry. He generally operates the cash register.

Apprentice Clerk: An apprentice clerk is an employee who has less than 2,080 hours of experience in the retail food industry. An apprentice clerk may perform the duties of any classification except managing clerk or head clerk.

Courtesy Clerk: A courtesy clerk is an employee who may perform only the following duties:

a. He may bag or box the merchandise after it has been checked out and take it to the customer's vehicle.

b. He may clean up the area between the front of the check stands and the entrances.

c. He may collect and line up push carts and return them to the store from the parking lot.

d. He may stock the bags in the check stand.

e. He may collect bottles, take them to the designated area, and sort them.

f. He may post and remove display signs.

Employees of Middlebrook Grocery Store and their present duties:

John Axel: John has always done the hiring and firing. He designs the work schedule for all the employees.

Ann James: Ann works as a checkout clerk. She has worked at Middlebrook for three years.

Jerry McIntosh: Jerry puts up the advertising signs, does the sweeping around the front of the store, and collects the grocery carts from the parking lot.

Wayne Phillips: Wayne was recently hired. He is just learning how to do the various jobs.

Tjoe Thian: Tjoe bags the groceries and carries them out to the customers' cars.

Mike Thomas: Mike drives to the farmers' market twice a week to select the fruits and vegetables for the store.

Rita Williams: Rita takes over making the work schedule and supervising employees when John is not there.

Yasuo Yagi: Yasuo assists Mike in selecting the fruits and vegetables at the farmers' market. He also places orders for the other items sold at the store.

A Report on Unionizing Middlebrook Grocery Store
Submitted by————

The employees of a unionized grocery store are generally classified into the

following categories:_____, _____,

_____, _____, _____,

_____, and _____. Each

category has its own duties and responsibilities. The managing clerk is the overall

director of the store. At Middlebrook, the employee who fits in this category is

_____. The senior head clerk is. . . .

SITUATION FIVE
The Anthropology Student

You are in an anthropology class. The class is studying the way time is viewed by various cultures. One of the texts for the course is Edward T. Hall's *The Silent Language,* which describes Americans' concept of time. Each student in the class has been asked to select a culture and write a brief paper on this culture's manner of viewing time. Since you are a foreign student, your teacher has asked you to report on your own country.

TASK

Write a paper that describes the manner in which your culture views time. Begin by classifying the various concepts of time in your culture. (You may use Hall's classification of time if it applies to your culture.) Then provide specific examples of common customs in the culture which illustrate each type of time.

Peer Correction of Student Compositions

The Anthropology Student

(1) The Japanese classified time by situation. (2) There are three types of time formal time which is based on a clock informal time which is the most common and typical but is not accurate or correct and Chinese animal time which uses the names of animals. (3) The first of all is formal time. (4) Many people use formal time in hospitals, schools, churches, and offices where they work. (5) The second is informal time, which came from ancestors of Japanese farmers. (6) It is the time which depends on nature such as the time when the sun rises and sets, the time when birds go home, and the time when morning glories bloom. (7) The third is Chinese animal time which people who did not have clocks invented many years ago by counting time according to the Chinese animals of year. (8) For example, cow time is 12 A.M. to 3 A.M. and tiger time is 3 A.M. to 6 A.M. (9) All three types of time are used in Japan for different uses and situations.

practice in correcting

The composition above has several errors in it. Follow the instructions below and correct the composition as directed.

Sentence 1: Use the present perfect tense.

Sentence 2: First add the necessary punctuation to the sentence. Then cross out any words or phrases that are redundant.

Sentence 3: Correct the phrase, "The first of all."

Sentence 4: Cross out any redundant words or phrases. Make the sentence passive.

Sentence 5: Add the necessary article.

Sentence 6: Cross out any redundant words or phrases.

Sentence 7: Cross out any redundant words or phrases. Add the necessary punctuation.

Sentence 9: Cross out any redundant words or phrases.

8

Defining by Comparison and Contrast

To *contrast* two items means to show how they are different; to *compare* two items, in a strict sense, means to show how they are similar. At times the two items that are being compared share much in common. For example, two restaurants, though they may differ in type of food and cost, both serve food to the public as a basis for business. An essay dealing with two restaurants will likely take many of the similarities for granted and focus instead on the differences. It is also possible to compare two items that have very little in common. For example, a beehive and an apartment building appear to have very little in common; yet if we examine their function and construction, we may discover several similarities. A paper dealing with these two items will typically emphasize their similarities since their differences are very obvious. An essay that points out the similarities between two very different items is called an *analogy.*

EXERCISE 8.1

grammatical focus: cohesive devices to replace nouns

When an item is referred to several times within the same paragraph, it is rather unusual to repeat the same noun over and over again. Instead, a writer can use other devices to make the paragraph cohesive or unified. The first, of course, is to use a pronoun.

The British were the earliest immigrants to the United States.
They came to escape religious persecution and to improve their economic condition.

Another is to repeat the noun.

The British were the earliest immigrants to the United States.
The British came to escape religious persecution and to improve their economic condition.

A third device is to use a synonym.

The British were the earliest immigrants to the United States.
The English came to escape religious persecution and to improve their economic condition.

A fourth technique is to replace the item with a term that describes the general class in which the item belongs.

The British were the earliest immigrants to the United States.
These settlers came to escape religious persecution and to improve their economic condition.

Finally, an item can be replaced with a very general term such as a person or group. Very often the general term is modified by an adjective which describes the writer's attitude toward the person, place, or object.

The British were the earliest immigrants to the United States.
These hardy people came to escape religious persecution and to improve their economic condition.

Notice that with the last two techniques the demonstrative pronoun *(these)* is used rather than the article. This is another cohesive device which can be used to link the second reference with the first reference to an item.

For each of the following sentences, indicate which of the following cohesive devices is used:

- Pronoun: P
- Repetition of the same word: R
- Synonym: S
- Class in which the item belongs: C
- General term: G

example:

___G___   *The American Indians* were the first inhabitants of the United States. *These sturdy people* were hunters, fishermen, and farmers.

_____   1. The chemical formula for *sucrose* is $C_{12}H_{22}O_{11}$. *It* is found in sugar cane and sugar beets.

_____   2. The chemical formula for *lactose* is also $C_{12}H_{22}O_{11}$. *This sugar* is found in milk.

_____   3. Ascorbic acid or *vitamin C* is found in fresh citrus fruits and vegetables. A lack of *this important element* can cause scurvy.

_____   4. Riboflavin or *vitamin B$_2$* is found in carrots, leafy vegetables, and yeast. A lack of *vitamin B$_2$* can cause slow growth and loss of weight.

_____   5. *The beam bridge* is the simplest kind of bridge. *It* consists of a long beam of timber or steel supported by piers.

_____   6. *The suspension bridge* is another type of bridge. *These spectacular structures* hang in the air from a pair of cables carried by two towers.

———— 7. *Earthenware* is easy to work and is fired at a relatively low temperature. *This pottery* must be glazed or given a glassy coating if it is to be used to hold liquids.

———— 8. *Stoneware* usually fires at a higher temperature than earthenware. Unlike earthenware, *stoneware* has a glasslike body and can therefore hold liquids without being glazed.

———— 9. *Petroleum* is a valuable raw material. *Crude oil* is a dark brown or black liquid which is made up of various kinds of hydrocarbons.

————10. *Natural gas* is also an important fuel. Like petroleum, *natural gas* is composed of hydrocarbons, which give off a great deal of heat when they burn.

EXERCISE 8.2

grammatical focus: cohesive devices to replace nouns

For each of the following sentences, fill in the blank with a cohesive device and label the device as in the previous exercise. Use each type of device at least one time. You may need to use more than one word in the blank.

example:

___P___ The central processing unit is the heart of the computer. ___It___ makes decisions, performs calculations, and controls the input and output units.

part one:

———— 1. *Ants* live in a complex society in which food exchange serves as a social bond. In order to communicate, _____bump into other ants and wave their antennas in the air.

———— 2. *Bees* also depend on food exchange as a source of social bond. _____ use dance pattern movements to tell other bees the direction, distance, and richness of the food.

_____ 3. *Hand drums* come in different sizes from less than 10 inches in diameter to 24 inches. _____are usually played with the hand although mallets, brushes, or sand blocks can be used.

_____ 4. *Tamborines* look like hand drums with added jingles around the shell. _____vary in size from 7 inches to 14 inches in diameter.

_____ 5. *Temporary drivers' licenses* are given to individuals after they pass the written test and the driving test. _____are good for 60 days.

_____ 6. *Regular drivers' licenses* are mailed to individuals within 60 days after they receive a temporary license. _____are good for a period of four years.

part two:

_____ 7. The first Indians to immigrate to the United States were *Sikhs*, from the Punjab in northwestern India. Many of _____worked on farms.

_____ 8. Many of the recent Indian immigrants are *students*. After receiving their degree, many of _____remain in the United States.

_____ 9. The first *Chinese* to reach the United States came during the California Gold Rush of 1849. Like many other people, _____came in search of gold.

_____10. In the 1860's many more *Chinese* arrived in California. Some of _____ worked to construct the first transcontinental railroad.

_____11. The first *Filipinos* to immigrate went to Hawaii. There, _____ worked as laborers on the sugar plantations.

_____12. In the 1920's many *Filipinos* immigrated to California. There, _____ worked as migrant agricultural workers.

_____13. Many *Mexicans* immigrated to the United States during the early twentieth century. _____readily found jobs in mining, railroading, and agriculture, but they were generally segregated from the rest of society.

_____14. Since World War II the condition of the *Mexicans* has improved. Today, many of _____have learned trade skills and obtained college degrees, so a middle-class has emerged.

_____15. After Fidel Castro came to power in 1959, the *Cubans* who immigrated consisted of rich people of the old elite. _____settled, by and large, in the Miami area.

_____16. After the failure of the Bay of Pigs in 1961, many of the *Cubans* who came to the United States were lower-middle class. _____too settled in the Miami area.

(Source of information: Anna Live and Suzanne Sankowsky. *American Mosaics*. Englewood Cliffs, N.J.: Prentice-Hall, Inc., 1980.)

EXERCISE 8.3

rhetorical focus: sentence connectors of comparison and contrast

mechanical focus: commas and semicolons with transitional phrases

There are many expressions in English that can be used to point out the similarity and differences between two items. Some of them are verbs, as in the following sentences.

- The origin of the immigrants to the United States *varies* from neighboring Central America to faraway Arctic lands.
- Early immmigrant groups tended to come from Europe, as *compared* with recent groups which tend to come from Asia and the Americas.
- The origin of early immigrant groups *contrasts* sharply with the origin of recent immigrant groups.

A second device for pointing out similarities and differences is coordinating words which give the two items equal emphasis. The following are common coordinating words.

- *Both* the early British settler *and* the recent Indochinese refugees immigrated to the United States for political reasons.
- Most immigrants *but* not all were able to adjust quickly to the new environment.

A third device that can be used for comparison and contrast is transition words. These words are used to introduce a new idea or to give an idea particular emphasis. When they are used to join two complete sentences, they are always preceded by a semicolon and followed by a comma. The following sentence illustrates some common transition words of comparison and contrast.

- Some immigrant groups were readily accepted in American society; *however, (on the other hand, in contrast,)* others have suffered much persecution.

A final technique for showing similarity and differences is use of subordinating words which are used to give less emphasis to one of the items being compared. Notice the difference in emphasis in the following sentences.

Although	*least emphasis*
Though	most immigrant groups have had to adjust to a new
Even though	language,
Whereas	*most emphasis*
While	the British settlers did not have to face this problem.

Although	*least emphasis*
Though	the British settlers did not have to adjust to a new language,
Even though	
Whereas	*most emphasis*
While	most immigrant groups have had to face this problem.

Since the subordinating words give less emphasis to an idea, it is important when using subordinating words to decide what you wish to emphasize. When a sentence begins with a subordinating word, the first clause is followed by a comma as is done in the sentences above. However, when the clause that is introduced by a subordinating word appears last, no comma is used.

	although
	though
Most immigrant groups have had to adjust to a new language	even though
the British did not face this problem.	whereas
	while

On a separate sheet of paper write a sentence that uses the listed expression of comparison and contrast. Be sure to refer back to Exercise 8.1 for the needed information.

example:

The chemical formula for glucose is $C_6H_{12}O_6$.
The chemical formula for sucrose is $C_{12}H_{22}O_{11}$.
Contrast the formulas of glucose and sucrose.
The chemical formula for glucose is $C_6H_{12}O_6$; on the other hand, the chemical formula for sucrose is $C_{12}H_{22}O_{11}$.

1. Compare the formulas for sucrose and lactose.

   The formula for both _____ and _____ is _____.

2. Contrast where sucrose and lactose are found.

   _____;

   in contrast, _____.

3. Contrast where vitamins C and B_2 are found and emphasize where vitamin C is found.

   Whereas _____,

   _____.

4. Contrast the results of a lack of vitamins C and B_2 and emphasize the result of a lack of vitamin B_2.

   Although _____,

   _____.

5. Contrast the construction of a beam bridge and a suspension bridge.

   _____;

   however, _____.

6. Indicate two ways in which earthenware and stoneware differ.

   _____ and _____ differ in _____ and

   _____.

7. Contrast the ability of earthenware and stoneware to hold liquids.

   _____,

   but _____.

8. Compare the composition of petroleum and natural gas.

Both _____ and _____

_____.

Use the information in Exercise 8.2, Part One, to write four additional sentences of comparison and contrast.

9. _____

_____

10. _____

_____

11. _____

_____

12. _____

_____

EXERCISE 8.4

rhetorical focus: analogies

An analogy depends on a comparison between two very different items. Sometimes the analogy is only one sentence. Many proverbs, for example, are one-sentence analogies. The following are some proverbs from different cultures. For each proverb write a sentence in which you indicate how the two items are similar.

proverb	similarity
Society is a barrel of apples.	In both a society and a barrel of apples, one unfit member can spoil the rest.

1. A good tongue is a good weapon.
2. A great fortune is a great slavery.
3. A happy marriage is a precious jewel.
4. A man's home is his castle.

5. Beauty is a blossom.
6. Fame is a magnifying glass.
7. Friendship is a fine crystal vase.
8. Knowledge is a treasure.
9. Money is the ace of trumps.
10. Promises are like pie crust.
11. Wise men in the world are like timber trees
    in a hedge.

Notice that many of the proverbs listed above compare an abstraction (*fame, promises*) with something concrete (*a magnifying glass, a pie crust*). Write five sentences in which you compare an abstraction with a concrete object. (You may, of course, use proverbs from your own language.) Then write a sentence in which you point out one similarity between the two items.

EXERCISE 8.5

rhetorical focus: parallel sentence structure
mechanical focus: semicolons joining sentences

One technique for providing unity in a paragraph that compares and contrasts two terms is to use the same sentence structure to explain each term. For example, in his "Letter from Birmingham Jail," Martin Luther King distinguished a just and unjust law. He explained some of the differences in the following way:

Any law that uplifts human personality is just. Any law that degrades the human personality is unjust.

Notice that the same sentence structure is used in both sentences. This technique emphasizes the difference between the two types of laws: while a just law *uplifts* the human personality, an unjust law *degrades* the human personality. In the same essay, Martin Luther King expressed his views on when each type of law should be obeyed:

One has not only a legal but a moral responsibility to obey just laws. Conversely, one has a moral responsibility to disobey unjust laws.

Notice again how the use of the same sentence structure emphasizes the significant differences between the two laws.

Two sentences that are closely related in meaning can be joined by a semicolon. By using a semicolon, a writer emphasizes the close relationship between the two sentences. Thus, King, for greater emphasis, could have joined the two sentences in the following way:

Any law that uplifts the human personality is just; any law that degrades the human personality is unjust.

Notice that when a semicolon is used, the second sentence does not begin with a capital.

The following pairs of terms are similar in meaning; however, they have different attitudes associated with them. Select *ten* pairs and for each pair write two sentences which explain one way in which the terms differ. Use the same sentence structure for both sentences and join some of them with a semicolon. You may, of course, consult the dictionary but try to describe in what sense you feel the terms are different.

example:

● A quiz, an exam

A quiz is a test I worry about the hour before; an exam is a test I worry about the week before.

1. an accident, a catastrophe
2. an acquaintance, a friend
3. an animal, a pet
4. an argument, a disagreement
5. a boat, a ship
6. a boss, a supervisor
7. a buck, a dollar
8. a car, a jalopy
9. a celebration, a party
10. a craft, a hobby
11. a clearance, a sale
12. a dream, a nightmare
13. a dress, a gown
14. a feast, a meal
15. a hike, a walk
16. a home, a house
17. a job, a profession
18. an old person, a senior citizen
19. a shop, a store
20. a speech, a talk

Reading Selection

The New Religion

As religion in America has become more secular, sport, perhaps the basic institution allowing for communal reaffirmation of secular values, has become more sacred. Sport manifests every characteristic of a formal, thriving religious movement. It has its gods (superstar athletes), its saints (those high-status sports figures who have passed to the great beyond—Lombardi, Rockne, Gipp, Thorpe), its scribes (the hundreds of sports reporters and sportcasters whose object is to disseminate the "word" of sports deeds and glories), its houses of worship (the Astrodome and other facilities that rival anything ever constructed to house traditional worship services). And sport has one other feature that traditional religion has long since lost in American society—massive throngs of highly vocal, maniacal "true believers" in the creeds and values relating to sport and its contribution to the maintenance of the "American way of life."

(Source: Harry Edwards. "Desegregating Sexist Sport," *Intellectual Digest*, November 1972, pp. 82–83.)

gloss:

- *secular:* not spiritual or religious
- *reaffirmation:* a second declaration
- *disseminate:* to spread
- *scribe:* a writer
- *maniacal:* insane

EXERCISE 8.6

1. The paragraph above presents an analogy between sport and religion. List the four areas in which Edwards compares the two.

   a.

   b.

   c.

   d.
   What additional feature does Edwards maintain that sport has?

2. Notice that since the third sentence is very long the author has repeated the same structures. What structures are repeated in this sentence?

3. The paragraph has many references to sport. What two cohesive devices does the author use in referring to this term?

Reading Selection

Parentage and Parenthood

It is apparently very necessary to distinguish between parenthood and parentage. Parenthood is an art; parentage is the consequence of a mere biological act. The biological ability to produce conception and to give birth to a child has nothing whatever to do with the ability to care for that child as it requires to be cared for. That ability, like every other, must be learned. It is highly desirable that parentage be not undertaken until the art of parenthood has been learned. Is this a counsel of perfection? As things stand now, perhaps it is, but it need not always be so. Parentage is often irresponsible. Parenthood is responsible. Parentage at best is irresponsibly responsible for the *birth* of a child. Parenthood is responsible for the development of a human being—not simply a child, but a human being. I do not think it is an overstatement to say that parenthood is the most important occupation in the world.

(Source: Ashley Montagu. *The American Way of Life.* New York: G.P. Putnam's Sons, 1967.)

EXERCISE 8.7

1. This passage distinguishes the meaning of two very similar terms. List the three contrasting definitions of parenthood and parentage that are contained in the text.

   a. parenthood is ———————————— parentage is ——————————

   b. parenthood is ———————————— parentage is ——————————

   c. parenthood is ———————————— parentage is ——————————

   Notice that the author uses parallel sentence structure to make these distinctions. What two types of punctuation are used in the text for these parallel sentences?

2. The paragraph makes several references to parentage and parenthood. What cohesive device does the author use to refer to these terms?

3. The dictionary defines both parenthood and parentage as the state of being a parent. The distinction made between them in the text reflects the opinion of the author and may not necessarily be shared by everyone. According to Montagu, which one is more valuable? What does he believe should be the relationship between the two?

Writing Tasks

□

SITUATION ONE
The Health Student

You are a student in a health class. Currently your class is studying the nutritional value of popular American foods. Your teacher has provided you with the chart and information listed on page 131 regarding popular American sandwiches. She has asked you to write a paragraph in which you indicate which of the sandwiches would be the best choice for lunch and which the worst.

□ TASK

First, study the chart and information listed below. Second, decide which criterion you think is most important in selecting a sandwich—protein value, vitamin and mineral content, calories, fats and carbohydrates, or cost. Finally, complete the assigned paragraph in which you compare and contrast the five sandwiches.

cost per pound of protein

Beef, beef and pork bologna	$19.75
Poultry bologna	9.97
Hot dog	13.85
American cheese	9.53
Hamburger	11.12
Tuna	9.08
Peanut butter	4.54

Common Luncheon Sandwiches

The selection of a luncheon menu can be an important nutritional decision. Sandwiches are a common lunch in America. Among some of the more popular sandwiches are bologna, hamburger, cheese, tuna, and peanut butter. These sandwiches, however, differ greatly in their nutritional value, calories, and cost. For example, (Finish this section by pointing out one contrasting example for each criterion.)

In my opinion, the most important element(s) to consider in selecting a lunch is/ are. . . .

Therefore, I believe the best choice for lunch would be _____

whereas the worst choice would be _____. A comparison of these two selections will clearly demonstrate the differences between the two.

A bologna sandwich vs. other sandwiches

The table shows how much of a 7- to 10-year old child's Recommended Daily Allowance (RDA) for a number of nutrients is provided by various sandwiches. RDA's are those set by the National Academy of Sciences/National Research Council. Table is based primarily on data from the USDA.

Legend: ● 100% or more RDA ◑ 25% RDA ○ 5% or less

Sandwich	Calories	Fat (gm.)	Carbohydrate (gm.)	Sodium (mg.)
3 oz. beef or beef-and-pork bologna on white bread with mustard	413	26	30	1305
3 oz. hamburger on bun, with catsup	378	19	25	408
3 oz. American cheese on white bread, with mayo.	554	39	27	1548
3 oz. tuna on white bread, with mayo.	402	20	26	894
2 tbsp. peanut butter on white bread	324	18	31	448

Nutrient columns shown as pie charts: Zinc, Phosphorous, Magnesium, Iron, Calcium, Vitamin C, Folacin, Vitamin B12, Vitamin B6, Niacin, Riboflavin, Thiamin, Vitamin A, Protein.

(Source: Copyright 1980 by Consumers Union of United States, Inc., Mount Vernon, NY 10550. Excerpted by permission from *Consumer Reports*, August 1980.)

(Finish the paper by comparing and contrasting what you consider to be the best and the worst luncheon selection. Finally, add a concluding sentence.)

SITUATION TWO
The Linguistic Student

You are a student in a linguistics class. Currently you are studying a unit on semantics, i.e., the meaning of words. You have been investigating synonyms and your teacher has pointed out that while some linguists believe there are many synonyms in English, other linguists argue that no two words ever have exactly the same meaning. In order to illustrate this point, your teacher has listed a series of synonyms and asked you to select one pair and describe how, in your opinion, their meanings differ.

☐ TASK

Select two synonyms. (You may choose two from the list in Exercise 8.5 but you are not limited to these.) Then consider in what ways the terms have different meanings for you. Finally, write a paragraph in which you distinguish the two terms. Use the passage by Montagu as a model and include several sentences with parallel structures. You may, as Montagu has done, conclude the essay by indicating which term you believe has more value.

SITUATION THREE
The International Student

You are an international student. You are taking a course in American history. Currently your class is studying the experience of various immigrant groups. Your teacher has emphasized the fact that immigrant groups have differed greatly in their reasons for coming to the United States, in their place of settlement, in their economic class, and in their work. He has asked you to write a short paper in which you point out some of these differences.

☐ TASK

Write one or two paragraphs in which you compare and contrast the immigrant experience of several ethnic groups. You may use the information provided in Exercise 8.2, Part Two, but be sure to add any additional information you have about the immigration of people from your own country. You might begin with the following statement: "The experience of immigrant groups to the United States has differed in a number of ways."

SITUATION FOUR
The Urban Planner

You are an urban planner. You are preparing a speech on urban living. In one section of the speech you intend to discuss apartment living. You have decided to use an analogy of a beehive to describe this type of living arrangement.

TASK

Begin by studying the visual of the apartment complex and beehive pictured on page 134. List the ways in which the construction of the two are similar. Consider the size of each compartment, its shape, uniqueness, and exposure to the outside. Then list the similarities between the inhabitants of a beehive and an apartment complex. Consider where the inhabitants work, whether they all have the same jobs, and what they do in their shelters.

You may find it helpful to use some of the following information on beehives in your analogy.

- A beehive is composed of vertical combs of horizontal cells.
- The hexagonal cells are composed of two sizes, one for the workers (females) and the other slightly larger for the drones (males).
- Within the combs, the honey is stored in the upper part or the part farthest from the entrance.
- Some of the worker bees are always stationed near the entrance of the hive to protect it from intruders. They will sting any stranger such as other bees or ants who attempt to enter the nest and steal honey.

Finally, write an analogy in which you compare an apartment complex with a beehive. You might begin with the statement: "Apartment complexes and beehives have several important similarities." Finish the paragraph by pointing out the similarities between the two. Use the passage by Edwards on The New Religion as a model. Be sure to use sentence connectors of comparison and parallel sentence structure. Wherever possible, vary the cohesive devices that you use.

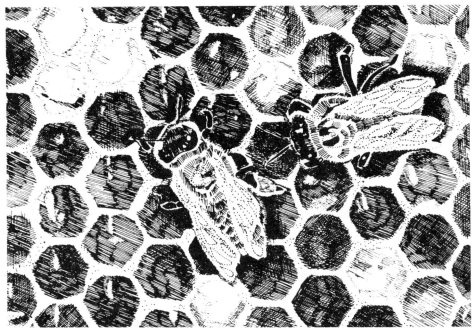

Peer Correction of Student Compositions

The International Student

(1) The experience of immigrant groups to the United States has differed in a number of ways. (2) The Chinese, for example, first reached the United States during the Gold Rush of 1849. (3) It was their search for wealth that caused them to migrate to the United States. (4) The Filipinos had a different reason for their migration into the United States. (5) The Filipinos came as laborers and the majority of the group worked on sugar plantations.

(6) In contrast from the Filipinos, the Cubans were rich people of the old elite. (7) The Cubans settled in the Miami area. (8) Whereas many Cubans came to establish a business many Filipinos came as laborers. (9) Mexicans, another immigrant group, moved into the United States searching for the jobs and better life. (10) Most of them settled in California.

(11) The last and final group is that of the Western Samoan people. (12) Today most of them consist of students who are only here in the United States to learn and get a college degree. (13) The Indian students can stay after getting a college degree; however, the Western Samoan students must all go back to their country to help its development.

(14) Even though in the past the different immigrant groups had different reasons for migration into the United States, today many groups share the same reasons.

practice in correcting

The composition above has several errors in it. Follow the instructions on page 136 to correct the composition.

Sentence 3: The following definition from the *American Heritage Dictionary* distinguishes the use of migrate, emigrate, and immigrate. *Migrate* is used with reference both to the place of departure and the destination and can be followed by *from* or *to.* It is said of persons, animals, and birds and sometimes implies lack of permanent settlement (notably seasonal movement). *Emigrate* pertains to a single move by persons and implies permanence. It has specific reference to the place of departure, emphasizes movement from that place, and is usually followed by *from*. *Immigrate* specifies a single move by persons and implies permanence. However, it refers to the destination, emphasizes movement there, and is followed by *to*. Select the most appropriate word for Sentence 3.

Sentence 4: Replace *migration* with a more appropriate word and correct the preposition error.

Sentence 5: Replace *the Filipinos* with another cohesive device.

Sentence 6: Correct the preposition error.

Sentence 7: Use another cohesive device to replace *The Cubans*.

Sentence 8: Revise the sentence to emphasize the reason for Cuban immigration. Supply the correct punctuation.

Sentence 9: Correct the preposition error and the article errors.

Sentence 11: Delete any unnecessary words.

Sentence 12: Delete any unnecessary words.

Sentence 13: Revise the sentence using *although* and supply the proper punctuation. Be sure to emphasize the condition of the Western Samoan students.

Sentence 14: Cross out any unnecessary words. Replace migration with a more appropriate word. Be sure to use the correct preposition with this word.

III

EXPRESSING
AN
OPINION

9. Expressing and Supporting
   an Opinion
10. Ranking
11. Speculating

9

Expressing and Supporting an Opinion

We all hold opinions about other people and their actions. Often others do not share our opinion and so we attempt to convince them that our opinion is correct. For example, suppose an office supervisor named Katie Walker believes that one of her employees, Craig Chun, should be promoted because of his unusual diligence. However, some other people in personnel do not share this view. Ms. Walker might try to convince others of Mr. Chun's diligence by relating several specific things he did which showed his diligence. Or she might refer to the comments of other people who share her opinion. Both of these techniques are common ways of supporting an opinion.

EXERCISE 9.1

grammatical focus: demonstratives as cohesive devices

Demonstratives *(this/that, these/those)* are one cohesive device that can be used to express an opinion. For instance, if Craig Chun were promoted, Ms. Walker might comment, *"That's* good news." In this case, *that* refers to the fact that Mr. Chun was promoted. Often *this* is used when a speaker is referring to something that she or he has said, whereas *that* is used to refer to something someone else has said. For example, if someone other than Ms. Walker announced the promotion, she might comment, *"That's* good news." However, if she announced it herself, she would likely say, *"This* is good news." When demonstratives are used to express an opinion, the plural forms *(these/those)* are not used, even when the opinion refers to two facts. Thus, even if Ms. Walker learned that Mr. Chun had been both promoted and given a bonus, she would still say, *"That's* good news."

Demonstratives are not always used to express an opinion; they can also be used to replace the pronoun *it*. Notice the following example.

Mr. Chun will move to a new office. *It* will be on the fourth floor.
Mr. Chun will move to a new office. *This* will be on the fourth floor.

In this example, *this* refers to the new office; it does not, of course, express an opinion.

The following statements were made by the superintendent of a school district. They indicate which programs in his district will be affected by the new budget. For each statement, add an opinion statement. Use *this* with the opinion of the superintendent, and *that* with the citizen's opinion.

example:

- Superintendent: "Computer terminals will be installed in all junior high schools for math instruction."
- Superintendent: "This will certainly improve the quality of math instruction."
- Citizen: "That will cost the district a great deal of money."

1. Superintendent: "The music programs in the school will be eliminated."

   Superintendent:

   Citizen:

2. Superintendent: "No new physical education equipment will be purchased."

   Superintendent:

   Citizen:

3. Superintendent: "ESL programs will be eliminated."

   Superintendent:

   Citizen:

4. Superintendent: "Teacher salaries will be increased."

   Superintendent:

   Citizen:

5. Superintendent: "Teacher aides will no longer be hired."

   Superintendent:

   Citizen:

6. Superintendent: "New science textbooks will be purchased for all the schools."

   Superintendent:

   Citizen:

7. Superintendent: "The drama program will be discontinued."

   Superintendent:

   Citizen:

8. Superintendent: "Carpeting will be installed in the schools."

   Superintendent:

   Citizen:

9. Superintendent: "Additional books will be purchased for the school libraries."

   Superintendent:

   Citizen:

10. Superintendent: "The school lunch program will be discontinued."

    Superintendent:

    Citizen:

EXERCISE 9.2

grammatical focus: subordinate clauses

mechanical focus: punctuation of subordinate clauses

One way to convince someone else to accept your opinion is to tell them your reason for holding your opinion. In supporting the promotion of Craig Chun, Katie Walker could merely say, "I think Craig Chun should be promoted." However, to be more convincing, she should add her reasons for holding this position. For example:

I think Craig Chun should be promoted because he has demonstrated outstanding diligence.

In this sentence there are two clauses: a main clause ("I think Craig Chun should be promoted") and a subordinate clause ("because he has demonstrated outstanding diligence"). The second part of the sentence is called a subordinate clause because, unlike the main clause, it is not a complete sentence. When a subordinate clause follows the main clause, no comma is necessary. However, if the subordinate clause begins the sentence, it must be followed by a comma.

Because Craig Chun has demonstrated outstanding diligence, I think he should be promoted.

When subordinate clauses are used to express a reason, they are generally introduced by *because, as,* or *since.*

A second way to express a reason is to use *because of* followed by a noun.

Because of Craig Chun's outstanding diligence, I think he should be promoted.
OR
I think Craig Chun should be promoted because of his outstanding diligence.

Notice that the reason can occur either before or after the main clause and that a comma is necessary if the reason appears before the main clause.

Add a reason to each of the opinion statements that you wrote in Exercise 9.1. Use a subordinate clause with *because, as,* or *since,* or *because of* followed by a noun.

example:

- Superintendent: "Computer terminals will be installed in all junior high schools for math instruction."
- Superintendent: "I believe this is a fine plan since it will improve the quality of math instruction.
- Citizen: "Because of the high cost, I do not think that is a good idea."

EXERCISE 9.3

grammatical focus: direct and indirect speech

mechanical focus: punctuation of quotations

Another way to support an opinion is to refer to the comments of others who share the same opinion. For instance, if one of Craig Chun's co-workers also thinks he should be promoted, his supervisor could refer to this fact as a way of strengthening her own opinion. Ms. Walker could *repeat* exactly what the co-worker said (direct speech) or *report* on what the co-worker said (indirect speech). In indirect speech the past tense is often used and the first person pronoun is replaced with the third person pronoun.

direct speech:

Jane Dobson, one of Craig Chun's co-workers, pointed out, "I think Craig is very dedicated to the company."

indirect speech:

Jane Dobson, one of Craig Chun's co-workers, pointed out that she thought Craig was very dedicated to the company.

Notice that the direct quotation is enclosed in quotation marks and the sentence begins with a capital. On the other hand, the indirect quotation is introduced with *that* and no quotation marks are used.

Each of the following statements expresses the opinion of a foreign student regarding Americans' view of time. Add the necessary punctuation and capitalization to each of the quotations; then change the sentence to indirect speech.

example:

biho cha stated i think americans are too concerned with the clock.
Biho Cha stated, "I think Americans are too concerned with the clock."
Biho Cha stated that he thought Americans were too concerned with the clock.

1. jeannie kwon said i believe americans think of time in terms of money.

2. guillermo lopez pointed out i think americans are proud that they are always so prompt.

3. peter tam stated i feel that americans concern for time makes the country operate efficiently.

4. rosa gomez stated i think that americans worry too much about being late.

5. susanna lau commented i like the fact that americans start things on time.

The following expressions can also be used to introduce direct quotations. They are not, however, used with indirect speech.

According to Biho Cha,
In the words of Biho Cha,
In the opinion of Biho Cha, } "Americans are too concerned with the clock."
As Biho Cha points out,
As Biho Cha says/notes/states,

Ask three of your classmates their opinion about Americans' view of time. Then write three direct quotations using the expressions listed above. Be sure to follow the expression with a comma.

6.

7.

8.

EXERCISE 9.4

rhetorical focus: expressions of opinion

An opinion statement can be expressed in several ways. One technique is to use a verb of belief as in the following example. (Notice that in these sentences the statement of belief is introduced by *that*.)

I believe/think/feel
It seems to me   } that Americans are too concerned with time.
It appears to me

A second way to express an opinion is to use an introductory phrase, such as the following. Notice that each of these expressions is followed by a comma and *that* is not used.

In my opinion,
In my view,
From my point of view,   } Americans are too concerned with time.
From my perspective,
As I view it,

A final technique to express an opinion is not to include any expression of belief. For example:

Americans are too concerned with time.

This is a very strong statement of belief. Sometimes statements like these are introduced with adverbs such as the following, which give the statement even greater emphasis.

Clearly,
Certainly,
Undoubtedly,   } Americans are too concerned with time.
Truly,

The following is a list of proverbs. For each proverb rewrite the sentence in your own words. Then add a sentence which expresses your opinion about the proverb. Use one of the expressions of opinion. Be sure to use each of the various types of opinion phrases.

example:

- Proverb: A friend is best found in adversity.
- Restatement: This proverb states that the best time to find out who your friends are is when you have problems.
- Opinion: From my perspective, this proverb is not an accurate view of friendship.

1. A good friend never offends.

   Restatement:

   Opinion:

2. A good name is better than riches.

   Restatement:

   Opinion:

3. A good servant makes a good master.

   Restatement:

   Opinion:

4. A good tale ill told is a bad one.

   Restatement:

   Opinion:

5. A little knowledge is a dangerous thing.

   Restatement:

   Opinion:

6. A man is not good or bad because of one action.

   Restatement:

   Opinion:

7. A man may live upon little, but he cannot live upon nothing.

   Restatement:

   Opinion:

8. A man may talk like a wise man and yet act like a fool.

   Restatement:

   Opinion:

9. A man's wealth is his enemy.

   Restatement:

   Opinion:

10. A quiet tongue shows a wise head.

    Restatement:

    Opinion:

11. A word hurts more than a wound.

Restatement:

Opinion:

EXERCISE 9.5

rhetorical focus: statements of reason

Subordinate clauses with *because, as,* and *since* are one way to express reasons. Another way to state a reason is to use a subordinate clause with one of the following phrases:

I believe / say / think this because. . . .
I feel this way because. . . .

If more than one reason for holding an opinion will be mentioned, sentences such as the following can be used.

I have several reasons for believing / saying / thinking this.
My reasons for believing / saying / thinking this are as follows.

Each of the reasons should then be introduced with phrases such as the following.

My first / second / reason is that. . . .
Third / Fourth, I believe / feel / think that. . . .
The final reason is that. . . .

Add your reasons for holding the opinion you expressed about each of the proverbs in Exercise 9.4. For at least two of the proverbs list more than one reason.

example:

- Proverb: A friend is best found in adversity.
- Restatement: This proverb states that the best time to find out who your friends are is when you have problems.
- Opinion: From my perspective, this proverb is not an accurate view of friendship.
- Reason: I say this because I believe friends can also prove themselves in times of joy.

Reading Selection

Americans and Time

Time talks. It speaks more plainly than words. The message it conveys comes through loud and clear. Because it is manipulated less consciously, it is subject to less distortion than the spoken language. It can shout the truth where words lie. . . .

Promptness is valued highly in American life. If people are not prompt, it is often taken either as an insult or as an indication that *they* are not quite responsible. There are those, of a psychological bent, who would say that *we* are obsessed with time. *They* can point to individuals in American culture who are literally time-ridden. And even the rest of us feel very strongly about time because we have been taught to take it so seriously. We have stressed this aspect of culture and developed it to a point unequaled anywhere in the world, except, perhaps, in Switzerland and north Germany. Many people criticize our obsessional handling of time. *They* attribute ulcers and hypertension to the pressure engendered by such a system. Perhaps *they* are right.

(Source: Edward Hall. *The Silent Language.* Greenwich, Conn.: Fawcett Publications, Inc. 1959, pp. 15, 21.)

gloss

- *manipulated:* handled
- *bent:* tendency
- *engendered:* produced

EXERCISE 9.6

The excerpt above expresses the opinion of Edward T. Hall, a noted anthropologist, regarding Americans' view of time.

1. The first paragraph expresses Hall's opinion of the power of time. Hall believes time can communicate even more accurately than the spoken language. Why does he believe this is so? What reason does he give for believing this? What structure does he use to provide his reason? The first paragraph has several references to time. Circle all the pronouns that refer to time in this paragraph.

2. In the second paragraph Hall discusses Americans' concern for promptness. According to Hall, who believes that Americans are obsessed with time? Hall states that some people believe that Americans' obsession with time causes ulcers and hypertension. Does Hall share this opinion? How does he express this opinion?

3. List the word or words that each of the underlined pronouns refers to.

reference

1. they   _____

2. we   _____

3. they   _____

4. they   _____

5. they   _____

Writing Tasks

SITUATION ONE
The American Studies Student

You are a student in an American Studies Class. Your class has just finished reading Edward T. Hall's *The Silent Language*. One of your assignments is to write a short paper in which you express your opinion regarding Hall's discussion of Americans' concern with promptness.

TASK

First, reread the excerpt from *The Silent Language*. Begin your essay by summarizing, in your own words, Hall's view of time as a form of communication and his belief about Americans' concern with promptness. After you have summarized Hall's position, indicate whether or not you agree with his opinion and list your reasons for either accepting or rejecting his views. Finally, give at least two specific examples to support your position. Describe at least two incidents from your own experience which show how Americans view promptness. Be sure to use the expressions of opinion and reason discussed in the chapter. Introduce your example with phrases such as, *for example, for instance,* or *to give an example.*

You are a foreign student advisor at a community college in the United States. You recently received a letter from a parent of one of your foreign students. He would like your opinion regarding his daughter's future plans at the college.

□ *TASK*

First, read the letter below. Then write a response to the letter. Be sure to state clearly what your opinion is regarding Maria's continued enrollment at the college. In addition provide several reasons for your opinion. Use the expressions of opinion and reason discussed in the chapter. Include the return address and the inside address as is done in the letter below.

12-97 Otwock
Lublin, Poland
January 17, 198–

Ms. Lisa Frieden, Foreign Student Advisor
Portland Community College
12000 SW 49th Avenue
Portland, Oregon 97219
USA

Dear Ms. Frieden,

My daughter, Maria Bukowski, is enrolled in the Business School at your college. She has just completed her first semester. Her letters to us indicate that she is having a great deal of difficulty. First, her English is not progressing well; in fact, she will have to repeat the English course she took last semester. She passed all of her business courses last semester, but she received a C or C– in all of them. She writes that the reason for her poor progress is that she is very homesick. There is no one else from our country on campus and she has not found it easy to make friends with Americans. She wants very much to return home.

Her mother and I think it is very important that she finish her schooling and receive a bachelor's degree from an American college. I have written her and told her I want her to stay for at least one more semester.

Maria tells me that you have been very helpful ever since she arrived. Since you know her and have spoken with her on several occasions, I would like to have your opinion regarding her continued enrollment. I look forward to receiving your letter.

Sincerely,

Mr. J. L. Bukowski

Mr. J.L. Bukowski

SITUATION THREE
The Political Science Student

You are a student in a political science class. Recently your class has been discussing various state laws which some people consider to be extremely unjust. Some of these laws, since they are very old, are no longer enforced; others are recent laws which are fully enforced. The following are a few of the state laws you have discussed.

1. A state law that forbids individuals who are not members of the Caucasian race from swimming in public swimming pools.
2. A state law that forbids the posting of public signs in any language other than English.
3. A state law that forbids the sale of laetrile, a drug some people believe is highly effective in fighting cancer.
4. A state law that makes the possession of one ounce of marijuana a felony (serious crime).
5. A state law that forbids smoking in designated public areas.

In view of these laws your professor has asked you to submit a paper in which you express your opinion regarding the following quotation.

In a play by Sophocles, a king who has created an unpopular law says the following:
"Whoever is chosen to govern should be obeyed. He must be obeyed. He must be obeyed in all matters whether the matters are just or unjust. Only a man who knows how to obey will ever know how to give commands when the time comes."

TASK

Write an essay in which you indicate whether or not you believe all laws must be obeyed. Give at least three reasons to support your opinion. You may, of course, refer to the laws listed above if they support your opinion. Be certain to use the phrases described in the chapter to introduce the various reasons that you provide.

SITUATION FOUR
The Industrial Relations Student

You are a student in an industrial relations class. Your class has just read the case described below regarding the firing of Christie Keyes. Your instructor has asked you to write a short paper in which you discuss whether or not you think the firing was fair.

TASK

Read the information listed below about Christie Keyes, a former employee of Kaiser Medical Foundation. Begin by summarizing the important facts in the case. Then indicate whether or not you believe the decision to fire her was fair. Be certain to list several reasons to support your opinion.

Union Contract—Kaiser Medical Foundation

According to the union contract, employees of Kaiser Medical Foundation have a right to three days off with pay at the time of their marriage. However, they must give their supervisor as much notice as possible so that arrangements can be made to cover their absence. Furthermore, whenever employees are absent, they must notify their supervisor at least 1½ hours before work begins.

Personnel Records—Christie Keyes

Christie Keyes worked for two years as a customer service representative at Kaiser Medical Foundation. The following are the facts regarding her firing.

On September 3, 198–, Ms. Keyes asked her supervisor, Mr. Bunch, if she could postpone her vacation from September to October because she was getting married. Mr. Bunch agreed to the change. However, on Friday, September 5, Ms. Keyes told Mr. Bunch that she wanted the following week off because she had some personal problems to think about. Mr. Bunch agreed to the change.

That Saturday Ms. Keyes decided to marry her fiancé and the wedding took place on the following day. Ms. Keyes did not tell her supervisor about the marriage until Friday, September 12. On this day, Ms. Keyes came in to see Mr. Bunch and asked for an extension of her vacation with three days of marriage leave. She explained that her mother did not know of her marriage and she wanted to visit her to tell her the news.

Mr. Bunch told her that another employee had been scheduled to be off on September 15, 16, and 17 so that this was not possible. However, he offered to change three of the days that Ms. Keyes took the week before from vacation to marriage leave. She could then keep three days of vacation for a later time. Ms. Keyes refused the offer and insisted that she must have September 15, 16, and 17 off. Mr. Bunch again pointed out that this was not possible.

Ms. Keyes decided to take September 15, 16, and 17 off to visit her mother even though she did not have permission to miss work. Ms. Keyes believed that her supervisor would know why she was not at work. Therefore, she did not contact him to explain the reason for her absence until Wednesday, September 17. When Ms. Keyes did call, Mr. Bunch told her that she had been fired for failing to show up at work for three days.

Peer Correction of Student Compositions

The American Studies Student

(1) Edward Hall, a noted anthropologist, expressed his opinion regarding Americans' view of time in the excerpt from *The Silent Language*. (2) He points out that Americans are concerned with promptness. (3) According to Hall's view of time, "Promptness is valued in America." (4) I agree on Mr. Hall that Americans were too concerned with time.

(5) The following is a few examples to support my point of view. (6) One day, one of my professors was very angry when the students started a conversation a minute before the class officially end. (7) He warned all the students, saying "Hey, I like to use every second of the fifty-minute lecture because I'm paid for every single minute. (8) Additionally, when my Calculus instructor comes late to class one day, he said: I'm sorry for being late," even though he was only five minutes late. (9) Also my friend who lives next door always says. "I don't have time for that," or "I'm sorry I wasted your time." (10) Finally, a couple who was invited to my house argued for a long time because the wife was late to the party for fifteen minutes. (11) The wife came from their home and he came from work. (12) He complained that she is always late even though she had already apologized to me.

(13) Americans are too concerned of time from my perspective. (14) They think of time as a very valued piece of jewelry.

practice in correcting

The composition on page 153 has several errors in it. Follow the instructions below and correct the composition as directed.

Sentence 2: Correct the errors in verb tense. Keep the sentence in the same tense as sentence 1.

Sentence 3: Correct the phrase that introduces the quotation. Change the quotation so that it is the exact words of the article.

Sentence 4: Correct the error in verb tense and choice of preposition.

Sentence 5: Correct the error in subject–verb agreement.

Sentence 6: Correct the error in verb tense.

Sentence 7: Add the necessary punctuation marks.

Sentence 8: Correct the error in verb tense and punctuation. Replace "additionally" with another sentence connector.

Sentence 9: Correct the error in punctuation.

Sentence 10: Correct the error in the choice of preposition.

Sentence 12: Correct the error in verb tense.

Sentence 13: Change the position of the opinion phrase and correct the error in the choice of preposition.

Delete any examples from the paragraph that do not directly support the idea that Americans are very concerned with promptness.

10

Ranking

To rank items is to put them in order of their importance. For example, suppose that the owner of a small restaurant has decided that the restaurant needs several things: a new microwave oven, a larger grill, new counter stools, and a new interior paint job. However, he cannot afford to have them all done immediately. Thus, he will likely decide which of the items is most necessary, next necessary, and so on. In determining which item is most critical, the owner probably has to weigh several factors. He has to decide whether it is more important to improve the speed of service by purchasing a new microwave oven and larger grill, or if it is more important to improve the physical appearance of the restaurant by buying new stools and repainting the walls. Until the owner decides which of these factors is most important for his business, it is difficult to make a decision as to which item to purchase first. The ranking of items, then, reflects the values or priorities of an individual. There is no right or wrong way of ranking items. A particular order is good only insofar as it satisfies the needs of an individual.

EXERCISE 10.1

grammatical focus: the expletive there

There is sometimes used as an adverb to indicate location.

The restaurant is over there.

At other times, *there* is used as an expletive, or a word that has little meaning but merely fills a position in a sentence.

There are several restaurants.

A sentence could even contain both uses of *there*.

There are several restaurants over there.

When *there* is used as an expletive with the verb *to be* and a noun, it can be followed by several structures which describe the noun.

1. An infinitive phrase
   There are many restaurants to choose from in the downtown area.
2. A relative clause
   There are three restaurants which serve fast food.
3. A present participial phrase or reduced clause
   There is one restaurant (which is) facing the lake.
4. A past participial phrase or reduced clause
   There are two restaurants (which are) advertised in the tourist guide.
5. A prepositional phrase or reduced clause
   There is one restaurant (which is) near the bus station.

If you had to select which restaurant to have lunch in, you would have to decide which factor is the most important to you. For example, if you were in a hurry, the fast food restaurant would probably be your first choice. On the other hand, if you felt like relaxing and going to a restaurant with a pleasant view, the restaurant facing the lake would probably be your first choice.

For each of the following categories write *at least two* sentences with the expletive *there* and a structure which describes the noun.

example:

- Infinitive: There are many homes to purchase in the area.
- Relative clause: There are some homes which are quite expensive.
- Present participial: There are other homes selling for under $78,000.
- Past participial: There are a few homes located near the shopping center.
- Prepositional phrase: There are several homes near the school.

1. Infinitive: There are many graduate schools to select from in the United States.

   Relative clause:

   Present participial:

   Past participial:

   Prepositional phrase:

2. Infinitive: There are many kinds of jobs to have.

   Relative clause:

   Present participial:

   Past participial:

   Prepositional phrase:

3. Infinitive: There are many classes to take at a university.

   Relative clause:

   Present participial:

   Past participial:

   Prepositional phrase:

4. Infinitive: There are many kinds of cities to live in around the world.

   Relative clause:

   Present participial:

   Past participial:

   Prepositional phrase:

5. Infinitive: There are many kinds of sports to play.

   Relative clause:

   Present participial:

   Past participial:

   Prepositional phrase:

6. Infinitive: There are many new and used automobiles to purchase.

   Relative clause:

   Present participial:

   Past participial:

   Prepositional phrase:

7. Infinitive: There are many types of entertainment to choose from.

   Relative clause:

   Present participial:

   Past participial:

   Prepositional phrase:

8. Infinitive: There are many kinds of people to meet.

   Relative clause:

   Present participial:

   Past participial:

   Prepositional phrase:

9. Infinitive: There are many kinds of supervisors to work for.

   Relative clause:

   Present participial:

   Past participial:

   Prepositional phrase:

10. Infinitive: There are many kinds of teachers to have.

    Relative clause:

    Present participial:

    Past participial:

    Prepositional phrase:

11. Infinitive: There are many places to spend a vacation.

Relative clause:

Present participial:

Past participial:

Prepositional phrase:

EXERCISE 10.2

grammatical focus: cleft sentences

In ranking items it is important to indicate on what basis the items are to be ranked. For example, there may be several sections of the same course offered at a university. For some students the most important factor in selecting a section might be the teacher and the least important might be the time that it meets. For other students these priorities might be just the opposite. One way to express your priorities is the following.

I believe the teacher is the most important factor to consider in selecting a class.

I think the time is the least important factor to consider in selecting a class.

One way to emphasize the fact that the teacher is what determines an individual's choice is to use a cleft sentence. A cleft sentence begins with *what* and ends with *the teacher*. A form of *to be* is also added before *teacher*. Circle these changes in the following example.

What I believe is the most important factor to consider in selecting a class is the teacher.

Placing *the teacher* at the end of the sentence puts greater emphasis on it. The same change could be made with the second sentence to emphasize the factor of time. Circle the changes that have been made in the following sentence.

What I think is the least important factor to consider in selecting a class is the time.

It is also possible to omit the expression of belief (*I believe, I think*) as in the following example.

What is the most important factor to consider in selecting a class is the teacher.

The following is a list of expressions that can be used in indicating priorities.

What is the (most) (important) (factor)   to (consider)
            (least) (essential) (thing)   (think about)
                  (critical) (element)
                       (standard)
                       (criterion)

Write two cleft sentences for each of the following items. In one sentence indicate what you consider the most important factor to consider in ranking the items and in the other indicate the least important factor. In one of these sentences include an expression of belief.

example:

- homes—in purchasing a home
- Highest priority: What is the most critical thing to consider in purchasing a home is cost.
- Lowest priority: What I feel is the least important factor to consider in purchasing a home is the arrangement of the rooms.

1. graduate schools—in selecting a graduate school

   Highest priority:

   Lowest priority:

2. jobs—in selecting a job

   Highest priority:

   Lowest priority:

3. classes—in selecting a class

   Highest priority:

   Lowest priority:

4. cities—in deciding which city to live in

   Highest priority:

   Lowest priority:

5. sports—in deciding which sport to play

   Highest priority:

   Lowest priority:

6. automobiles—in deciding which automobile to purchase

   Highest priority:

   Lowest priority:

7. entertainment—in deciding which kind of entertainment to select

   Highest priority:

   Lowest priority:

8. people—in selecting a friend

   Highest priority:

   Lowest priority:

9. supervisors—in determining the effectiveness of a supervisor

   Highest priority:

   Lowest priority:

10. teachers—in determining the effectiveness of a teacher

    Highest priority:

    Lowest priority:

11. vacation plans—in selecting a vacation place

    Highest priority:

    Lowest priority:

EXERCISE 10.3

grammatical focus: parallel structure: not only . . . but also

Individuals may, of course, have more than one reason for ranking items in a certain order. For example, an individual may believe that in selecting a home two factors are of equal importance: cost and location. These criteria could be expressed by simply joining them with *and*.

In selecting a home both cost and location are important.

Another way of joining the two standards is to use *not only . . . but also*.

In selecting a home not only is cost important but also location.

Writing it this way gives greater emphasis to the criteria of location. It suggests either that the author has already discussed the standard of cost or that most people readily accept cost as important. Notice in the sentence that the main verb *(is)* precedes *cost.*

Write a sentence with *not only . . . but also* to indicate which factors you think are important in selecting the following items.

example:

a home—In selecting a home not only is initial cost important but also the mortgage interest rate.

1. clothes

2. furniture

3. a grocery store

4. a book

5. a movie

6. a restaurant

7. a job

8. a doctor

9. a husband / wife

10. a university

EXERCISE 10.4

rhetorical focus: expressing priorities

Answer each of the following questions by ranking the items according to your preferences. Remember there is no right or wrong answer; it is merely what you prefer. Then write a sentence that expresses your preference. Use a cleft sentence, or if you have two factors of equal importance, use *not only . . . but also.* You may use any of the following patterns:

- What I would prefer to do is . . .
- What I feel / believe / think / is most important in ———— is . . .
- I would prefer not only to ————, but also to . . .

- I feel / believe / think that in ———— it is important to consider not only ———— but also. . .

Finally add a sentence which expresses your reasons for your preference.

example:

Which factor do you believe is most important in selecting an apartment?

    __1__   rent
    __2__   location
    __1__   length of lease
    __3__   condition of the building

I think that in selecting an apartment it is important to consider not only the rent but also the length of the lease. I feel this way because I usually do not stay in one place for more than one year.

1. What would you prefer to do in your free time?

    ———————— listen to music

    ———————— play sports

    ———————— read

    ———————— talk with friends

    ———————— watch TV

2. What do you think is the most important thing to consider in selecting a class?

    ———————— the course requirements

    ———————— the other students

    ———————— the teacher

    ———————— the textbook

    ———————— the time it meets

3. Which factor do you think is most important in purchasing a car?

    ———————— the color

    ———————— the cost

    ———————— the horsepower

———— the manufacturer

———— the safety

4. Which factor do you think is most important in selecting a job?

———— the amount of supervision

———— the location

———— the permanence of the job

———— the possibility for promotion

———— the salary

5. Which field would you prefer to study?

———— humanities

———— math

———— philosophy

———— physical science

———— social science

6. Which problem do you believe is the most serious for a country?

———— crime

———— discrimination

———— inflation

———— poverty

———— transportation

7. Which factor do you think is most important in selecting a restaurant?

———— the atmosphere

———— the cost

———— the quality of service

———— the quality of food

———— the variety of food

8. What do you prefer to do least?

———— cook

———— exercise

———— read

_____ shop

_____ study

9. Which would you prefer to take to travel in a country?

_____ a bus

_____ a motorcycle

_____ a private automobile

_____ a taxi

_____ a train

10. To which program would you prefer to give additional federal funds?

_____ defense

_____ education

_____ medical care

_____ space exploration

_____ welfare

Reading Selection

Teachers

Teachers need more than a knowledge of subject matter and a little practice teaching experience before they enter the classroom. They need knowlege *about* knowledge, about the ramifications of the subject or subjects they teach, about how those subjects relate to other subjects and to knowledge—and life—in general. They need insights into their purposes as a teacher—why they are teaching what they are teaching, and how these purposes relate to the institutional setting of the school and to the values of the local community and the society at large. They need understanding of the processes of growth and development and of the nature of mind and thought. Most important, perhaps, they need to know that they need to know these things—they need to understand the kinds of questions their teaching will raise and to have some sense of where to turn for further understanding.

(Source: Charles Silberman. *Crisis in the Classroom.* New York: Random House, 1970, pp. 489–90.)

gloss

• ramifications: consequences

EXERCISE 10.5

1. In the selection, Silberman discusses what knowledge he believes teachers need to have before they enter the classroom. List the four major things that Silberman believes teachers need to know.

   a.

   b.

   c.

   d.

   Which of these things does Silberman believe is the most important? Circle the phrase that is used to indicate this. In order to unify the paragraph, Silberman repeats the same phrase ("Teachers need..." or "They need..."). Underline all the uses of this phrase.

2. List six characteristics that you believe a person must have in order to be an effective teacher, such as patience or intelligence. Then select the one that you feel is the most important. Finally write a brief paragraph in which you describe these characteristics. Use a parallel structure such as Silberman has done (e.g., "Teachers should be...," "They should..."). Finally, indicate which you think is the most important characteristic and why.

Writing Tasks

☐ SITUATION ONE
The Premed Student

You are applying to enter medical school. Part of the application requires that you write a short essay in which you indicate which characteristics you believe are most important to be a successful doctor.

☐ *TASK*

Begin by ranking the characteristics listed on page 167 according to which you believe are most necessary for a successful doctor. Be certain to add to the list any additional characteristics you think are important. Then write an essay in which you indicate the top *three* characteristics along with the least important characteristic. For each one of these give your reasons for ranking it in the order you did. Use cleft sentences and expressions of belief and reason.

———— diligence

———— efficiency

———— empathy

———— gentleness

———— integrity

———— intelligence

———— patience

———— other (specify) ————————————

———— other ————————————————

———— other ————————————————

SITUATION TWO
The Advertising Agent

You work in the advertising department of a bicycle manufacturer. Because of the energy shortage, your supervisor has asked you to design a brochure which urges people to purchase a bicycle for commuting purposes. You especially want to inform consumers as to what are the most important factors to consider in purchasing a bicycle.

TASK

Begin by ranking the characteristics listed below according to which you feel are the most necessary to have on a bicycle that will be used for commuting purposes. (Add any additional features you think are important.) Then write an essay in which you inform consumers what the *three* most important things are to consider in selecting a bicycle. Be sure to explain the reasons why each of these three features would be important to someone who would use the bicycle every day for a fairly long distance.

———— braking control

———— color

———— ease of pedaling

_____ ease of repair

_____ ease of shifting

_____ number of gears

_____ price

_____ seat comfort

_____ size

_____ strength of frame

_____ weight

_____ other (specify)_____

_____ other_____

_____ other_____

SITUATION THREE
The Taxpayer

Recently there has been much discussion about the problem of inflation. Congress is now considering a major cutback in the federal budget to help control the problem. Various federally funded programs will be severely cut. As a taxpayer, you have definite ideas as to which programs should be maintained and which should be cut. You have decided to write a letter to your Congressman expressing your views.

☐ TASK

Begin by ranking the federally funded programs according to which you believe should have continued federal support. Then write a letter to your Congressman in which you indicate which two programs should be cut and which two should not be cut. Be certain to provide your reasons for each. Address the letter to your local Congressman and use the structures discussed in Chapters Nine and Ten (cleft sentences, parallel structure and subordinate clauses, as well as expressions of belief and reason).

_____ agricultural assistance

_____ arts and humanities research

_____ defense

_____ education

_____ energy

_____ health care

_____ postal service

_____ science research

_____ Social Security

_____ space exploration

_____ urban development

_____ veterans assistance

SITUATION FOUR
The Second Language Student

You are studying English as a second language. Since you have a very good mastery of English, your teacher is curious to know what characteristics you believe are important in learning another language. He has asked you to write a brief essay in which you describe at least *three* characteristics that you think are important in mastering a second language.

TASK

First rank the characteristics listed below according to their importance when one is learning another language. Be certain to add any other characteristics you believe are necessary. Then write an essay in which you indicate at least *three* characteristics that you feel are important in learning a language and explain your reasons for including each of them. Wherever possible refer to your own experience as a second language learner. Use the structures discussed in Chapters Nine and Ten (cleft sentences, parallel structures and subordinate clauses, as well as expressions of belief and reason).

_____ ability to discriminate different sounds

_____ ability to memorize grammatical rules

_____ ability to memorize vocabulary

_____ avoidance of making errors

_____ high motivation to learn the language

_____ successful mastery of another foreign language

_____ willingness to make errors and experiment with the language

_____ willingness to use the language with native speakers

_____ youth

_____ other (specify)_____

_____ other_____

_____ other_____

_____ other_____

Peer Correction of Student Compositions

The Premed Student

(1) To be a successful doctor is one of my dreams. (2) What I believe is the most important factors to consider being a successful doctor are intelligence, diligence, and responsibility.

(3) First of all, intelligence is the most important characteristic which a student need to succeed in medical school. (4) Since medical science is one of the most complicated areas to study he should be intelligence enough to get into medical school.

(5) What I feel the next most important characteristic is diligent. (6) Because so much hard work is required in medical school a student has to have diligence. (7) A student must complete medical school within the certain period. (8) If he has no diligence, he won't complete his studies successfully.

(9) Not only diligence is important but also responsibility. (10) It seems to me if a doctor has no sense of responsibility, he surely cannot be a competent physician since the doctor has to deal with human life and death. (11) These three characteristic are the most important to success as a doctor.

(12) Finally, what I believe the least important factor is the location where a doctor practices. (13) Location is not essential if a doctor's motto is to serve the people. (14) The doctor should never hesitate to serve people everywhere.

practice in correcting

The composition on page 170 has several errors in it. Follow the instructions and correct the composition as directed.

Sentence 2: Correct the error in subject–verb agreement. Add a preposition which has been omitted.

Sentence 3: Correct the error in subject–verb agreement.

Sentence 4: Use the correct form of *intelligence*. Add the necessary punctuation.

Sentence 5: Add a verb which has been omitted. Use the correct form of *diligent*.

Sentence 6: Add the necessary punctuation.

Sentence 7: Correct the article error.

Sentence 9: Revise the word order so it is correct.

Sentence 10: Correct the article error.

Sentence 11: Correct the error in subject–verb agreement. Correct the preposition error.

Sentence 12: Add a verb which has been omitted.

Sentence 14: Correct the article error.

11

Speculating

To speculate is to reflect on a topic and perhaps make predictions about it. Quite often speculating begins by assuming that things are different than they really are. For example, you might imagine a situation in which it were possible to learn a second language by merely being hypnotized and told you knew the language. If this were indeed possible, you might speculate as to what you would do or how you would feel. Speculating on such possibilities, then, involves assuming that things are different than they are and then reflecting on what would be the effect of such changes.

EXERCISE 11.1

grammatical focus: conditional sentences

mechanical focus: commas with conditional sentences

Sometimes speculating involves reflecting on future possibilities. For example, a doctor might speculate on the possibility of being able to transplant a human brain. One way to express the possible effects of such a situation is to use conditional sentences such as the following.

If it is possible to transplant the human brain, this procedure will raise many ethical problems.

OR

If it were possible to transplant the human brain, this procedure would raise many ethical problems.

Notice that in order to indicate that such a development is a possibility, either the present or past tense of the verb is used in the *if*-clause (*if it* **is** *possible, if it* **were** *possible*). Notice also that with a third person singular subject, *were* is preferred in formal writing rather than *was*. Finally, with conditional sentences when the present tense is used in the *if*-clause, *will* is often used in the main clause; however, when the past tense is used in the *if*-clause, *would, might,* or *could* is frequently used in the main clause. The sentences above use *this procedure* in the main clause. It is also possible to use the expletive *there* and the simple form of the verb *to be,* as for example:

If it is possible to transplant the human brain, there will be many ethical problems.

OR

If it were possible to transplant the human brain, there would be many ethical problems.

Using the expletive *there* suggests that the author is more certain of the effects of the situation. Notice that a comma is always used after the *if*-clause.

Speculate about the possible effects of each of the following situations. Since the situations are all possibilities, use the present or past tense in the *if*-clause. In the main clause use either *there* or *this* plus a noun.

example:

- Situation: Suppose car manufacturers design an inexpensive electric automobile.
- Possible effect: If car manufacturers design (designed) an inexpensive electric automobile, there will (would) be less of an energy shortage.

  OR

  If car manufacturers design (designed) an inexpensive electric automobile, this invention will (would) reduce the energy shortage.

1. Situation: Suppose most businesses in the United States adopt a four-day work week.

   Possible effect:

2. Situation: Suppose consumers can do all their shopping by computer.

   Possible effect:

3. Situation: Suppose the United States prohibits any further immigration.

   Possible effect:

4. Situation: Suppose we establish a community on another planet.

   Possible effect:

5. Situation: Suppose the medical profession discovers a cure for cancer.

   Possible effect:

In each of the sentences listed above, the *if*-clause is in the active voice (*If car manufacturers design an inexpensive electric automobile*). However, when it is not necessary to include the agent, because the agent is either understood or not known, the passive voice is used in the *if*-clause (*If an inexpensive electric automobile is designed*). Write a conditional sentence for each of the following situations. Use the passive voice in the *if*-clause.

6. Situation: Suppose scientists discover life on other planets.

   Possible effect:

7. Situation: Suppose people deplete all the current sources of energy.

   Possible effect:

8. Situation: Suppose a computer company designs a computer to translate spoken language instantly.

   Possible effect:

9. Situation: Suppose the major powers accept a complete nuclear disarmament agreement.

   Possible effect:

10. Situation: Suppose all the major cities in the United States close the public schools.

    Possible effect:

It is also possible to speculate about things that have already occurred. For example, you might speculate how your life would have been different if you had never studied English. When conditional sentences are used to describe something that has already occurred, the past perfect tense (*had* + the past participle) is used in the *if*-clause and *would* plus the present perfect tense (*have* + the past participle) is used in the main clause.

If I had never learned English, I would never have come to the United States.

For each of the following situations write a conditional sentence with the past perfect and present perfect tense.

11. Situation: Suppose the automobile had never been invented.

    Possible effect:

12. Situation: Suppose the United States had adopted German as the national language.

    Possible effect:

13. Situation: Suppose the New World had never been discovered.

    Possible effect:

14. Situation: Suppose the printing press had never been invented.

    Possible effect:

15. Situation: Suppose the nuclear bomb had never been invented.

    Possible effect:

Write five additional sentences that describe either a possible situation or an unreal situation. Then ask one of your classmates to speculate on the possible effects of these situations.

EXERCISE 11.2

rhetorical focus: expressing hypothetical situations

A hypothetical situation is one that is not real. One way to describe these kinds of situations is to use *suppose* in the imperative as was done in the last exercise. Other common expressions to describe a hypothetical situation are *assume that* and *imagine that*. Sometimes the description of a hypothetical situation can be several sentences long. For example, the following excerpt by Marya Mannes from the book *But Will It Sell* is three sentences long.

Suppose there were no critic to tell us how to react to a picture, a play, or a new composition of music. Suppose we wandered innocent as the dawn into an art exhibition of unsigned paintings. By what standards, by what values would we decide whether they were good or bad, talented or untalented, success or failure?

Notice that the description of the hypothetical description ends with a question which is designed to explore the effects of the situation.

For each of the following hypothetical situations, add a sentence which further defines the context. (The sentence need not begin with *suppose.*) Then add a question which explores the effects of this situation. If it is possible that the situation can occur, use the present or past tense. If the situation is something that could not occur, use the past perfect and present perfect tense.

example:

Suppose that John F. Kennedy had not been elected President of the United States.

- Additional detail: Assume instead that Richard Nixon had been elected.
- Question of effect: How would this have changed United States history?

1. Assume that the institution of marriage no longer exists.

   Additional detail:

   Question of effect:

2. Suppose that there is a drug to make people young again.

   Additional detail:

   Question of effect:

3. Suppose the world's supply of water were depleted.

   Additional detail:

   Question of effect:

4. Assume that we had a world government.

   Additional detail:

   Question of effect:

5. Imagine that the telephone had never been invented.

   Additional detail:

   Question of effect:

6. Assume that the South had won the U.S. Civil War.

   Additional detail:

   Question of effect:

7. Imagine that there had never been any organized religion.

   Additional detail:

   Question of effect:

8. Suppose that the television had never been invented.

   Additional detail:

   Question of effect:

Describe three additional hypothetical situations using two statements of explanation and a question of effect. Then ask one of your classmates to answer these questions and the ones listed above.

EXERCISE 11.3

rhetorical focus: expressions of cause and effect
mechanical focus: commas and semicolons with transitional phrases

One way to express the possible effects of a hypothetical situation is to use verbs of cause and effect such as the following.

Assume that citizens were no longer required to pay federal taxes.

1. This would drastically *affect* the federal government.

2. This would *cause* the federal government to go bankrupt.

3. This would *create/produce/result in* the bankruptcy of the United States.

A second possibility is to use the subordinator *so that,* as in the following example.

(main clause)
Assume that citizens were no longer required to pay federal taxes
so that the federal government went bankrupt.
(subordinate clause)

Notice in this sentence that there is a main clause and a subordinate clause.

A final possibility is to use a transitional phrase, as in the following example.

(main clause)
Assume that citizens were no longer required to pay taxes; as a result,
(hence,/therefore,/thus,) the federal government went bankrupt.
(main clause)

Notice that in this example there are two main clauses. Because the sentence contains two main clauses, a semicolon is used after the first main clause and a comma is used after the transitional phrase *(as a result, hence, thus).*

Write three statements of effect for each of the hypothetical situations listed below. In one statement use a verb of cause and effect, in the second use the subordinator *so that,* and in the final sentence use a transitional phrase of cause and effect. Be sure to use the same verb tense as in the first sentence.

example:

Assume that the federal government went bankrupt.

- Verb of cause and effect: This would cause the federal government to collapse.
- *so that:* Assume that the federal government went bankrupt so that the government collapsed.
- Transitional phrase: Assume that the federal government went bankrupt; as a result, the government collapsed.

1. Assume that the federal government collapsed.

   Verb of cause and effect:

so that:

Transitional phrase:

2. Imagine that there were no exceptions to the grammatical rules of English.

Verb of cause and effect:

so that:

Transitional phrase:

3. Assume that all universities do away with letter grades.

Verb of cause and effect:

so that:

Transitional phrase:

4. Suppose there were no such thing as money.

Verb of cause and effect:

so that:

Transitional phrase:

5. Assume that everyone worked during the hours they wanted.

Verb of cause and effect:

so that:

Transitional phrase:

6. Imagine that the light bulb had never been invented.

Verb of cause and effect:

so that:

Transitional phrase:

7. Suppose that Lincoln had not freed the slaves.

Verb of cause and effect:

so that:

Transitional phrase:

8. Assume that penicillin had never been invented.

Verb of cause and effect:

so that:

Transitional phrase:

9. Assume that the United States had lost the Revolutionary War.

   Verb of cause and effect:

   so that:

   Transitional phrase:

10. Imagine that the computer had never been developed.

    Verb of cause and effect:

    so that:

    Transitional phrase:

Reading Selection

What's Worth Knowing?

Suppose all of the syllabi and curricula and textbooks in the schools disappeared. Suppose all of the standardized tests—city-wide, state-wide, and national—were lost. In other words, suppose that the most common material impeding innovation in the schools simply did not exist. Then suppose that you decided to turn this "catastrophe" into an opportunity to increase the relevance of the schools. What would you do?

We have a possibility for you to consider: suppose that you decide to have the entire "curriculum" consist of questions. These questions would have to be worth seeking answers to not only from your point of view but, more importantly, from the point of view of the students. In order to get still closer to reality, add the requirement that the questions must help the students to develop and internalize concepts that will help them to survive in the rapidly changing world of the present and future.

Obviously, we are asking you to suppose you were an educator living in the second half of the twentieth century. What questions would you have on your list?

(Source: Neil Postman and Charles Weingartner. *Teaching as a Subversive Activity.* New York: Delacorte Press, 1969, p. 59.)

EXERCISE 11.4

1. In the first paragraph the author describes a hypothetical situation. What structure is repeated to describe this situation? Underline the sentence that is used to explore the effects of the situation. Why do the authors put quotation marks around *catastrophe?* What do you think is the authors' attitude toward existing textbooks and tests? What makes you think so?

2. In the second paragraph the authors add two additional details to their hypothetical examples. What are they? According to the authors, whom should the questions satisfy? What must these questions do?

3. Paragraph 3 summarizes the purpose of the hypothetical situation. The authors want the reader to list the questions that they believe are worth exploring. Answer the authors' question, "What questions would you have on your list?" Make a list of at least eight questions that you believe would be worth seeking answers to.

Writing Tasks

SITUATION ONE
The Travel Agent

You are a travel agent. You are writing a brochure to advertise a vacation tour to Hawaii. You have decided to use a hypothetical situation to get the readers' attention before providing the details of the tour package.

TASK

Write two paragraphs of the brochure. In the first paragraph describe the following hypothetical situation. Ask your readers to imagine themselves relaxing on a Hawaiian beach and enjoying a vacation there. Continue describing several things they could do in Hawaii. Then ask your readers what they would do if there were an inexpensive five-day trip to Hawaii. In this paragraph use hypothetical expressions (*suppose, assume that, imagine that*) and conditional sentences.

In the second paragraph describe the details of your vacation package. Indicate the total cost and what is included in this price. You might describe several special features in the package such as a hotel on the beach, a champagne flight, one day free car rental, and so on.

SITUATION TWO
The Mayor

You are the mayor of a rather large U.S. city. In two weeks the residents will vote on whether or not to approve Proposition C which would raise their property taxes by 33 percent. Many citizens, of course, are strongly opposed to such a substantial increase in their taxes. However, as mayor, you realize that unless this proposition is passed, drastic cuts will have to be made in city services. You have decided to write a letter to your constituents urging them to vote yes on Proposition C.

☐ TASK

Write a letter to your constituents. Begin by describing a hypothetical situation. Ask the citizens to consider what it would be like to live in a city without police and fire protection, garbage service, mass transportation, public schools, libraries, and hospitals. Then discuss what effect the defeat of Proposition C would have on these public services. Close by urging them to vote yes on this proposition.

☐ SITUATION THREE
The Ecology Student

You are a student in an ecology class. Your professor has asked you to write an essay on a natural resource that is currently being depleted and to speculate on what effect the depletion of this resource would have on society. You have decided to write on the depletion of the water supply.

☐ TASK

Write the essay for your ecology class. Begin by describing the current depletion of water supply in the United States. Use some or all of the following facts.

- One-quarter of the water that the United States uses is taken from an ancient network of underground aquifers (water-bearing rock formations).
- The vast underground reserves of water have been seriously depleted in the last several decades. In 1950 the United States took 12 trillion gallons of water out of the ground; by 1980 the number of gallons doubled.
- As fresh water moves out of aquifers, salt water seeps in. Water containing 3 percent sea water is undrinkable.
- Many rivers and lakes are polluted with acid rain, pollution chemicals, and bacteria from sewage.
- It takes 14,935 gallons of water to grow a bushel of wheat, 60,000 gallons to produce a ton of steel, and 126 gallons to produce one egg.
- The United States uses approximately 80 percent of its water for agriculture, 15 percent for manufacturing, and 5 percent for domestic use.

(Source of information: "The Browning of America," *Newsweek*, February 23, 1981, pp. 26–37.)

In the second paragraph speculate as to what would happen if the water supply were severely depleted. What would be the effect on agriculture, manufacturing, and ultimately on people? Use hypothetical expressions, conditional sentences, and expressions of cause and effect.

SITUATION FOUR
The History Student

You are in an American history class. Your class has just finished studying the Civil War and is taking an exam on the topic. One of your essay questions asks you to speculate on what some of the effects would have been if the Confederacy had won the Civil War.

☐ TASK

Write a response to this exam question. Begin the essay with a statement of speculation using *suppose, assume,* or *imagine.* Follow this with a question that explores the possible effects of the South's winning the Civil War. Finish the paragraph by using some or all of the following information. Since the situation is no longer possible, use conditional sentences with the past perfect and present perfect tense.

Historical fact	Likely alternative if the Confederacy had won the Civil War
Lincoln is reelected.	Jefferson Davis is elected President.
The slaves are freed.	The slaves are not freed.
The Capitol is located in Washington, D.C.	The Capitol is located in Richmond, Virginia.
A strong central government is established. The state governments have less power.	A weak central government is established. The state governments have equal power.
Tariffs are imposed on manufactured goods to protect northern manufacturing interests.	Tariffs are not imposed on manufactured goods to promote the sale of agricultural products.

Peer Correction of Student Compositions

The Travel Agent

(1) Imagine that you are spending a sunny afternoon lying in a white sand beach under the sun and sipping the cold coconut juice through a straw. (2) While you are having sunbath, the breeze will cool you off. (3) When you close your eyes and listen, you will hear the natural music of the waves. (4) After a nap in this relaxing afternoon, you are ready to join the beautiful Hawaiian dancers to do the traditional Hawaiian dances. (5) When you get hungry, you can also try out some typical Hawaiian food.

(6) This is not a dream. (7) You can make this come true by just visiting one of our travel agency. (8) We are offering a vacation package to Maui which will have all this fun with a low cost. (9) This is a five-days tour which contain the round trip flight ticket and five nights at a hotel. (10) Since Easter holiday is coming up, we would have a big surprise for you. (11) Now you can also dine at the Hilton Hotel. (12) You can enjoy your dinner under the candlelight with a famous band playing some soft band music. (13) For all this, you have to pay only $700. (14) But hurry, since we do not have many seats. (15) If you reserve now, you would have a better chance to get in on our special vacation package. (16) Bon voyage.

practice in correcting

The composition above has several errors in it. Follow the instructions and correct the composition as directed.

Sentence 1: Correct the preposition and article errors. Delete any unnecessary words.
Sentence 2: Correct the error in verb tense. Keep the example in the present tense. Correct the article error.
Sentence 3: Correct the error in verb tense.
Sentence 4: Correct the preposition error. Delete any unnecessary words.

Sentence 7: Use the correct form of *agency*.

Sentence 8: Correct the preposition error.

Sentence 9: Use the correct form of *days*. Correct the error in subject–verb agreement and article.

Sentence 10: Correct the error in verb tense and article.

Sentence 12: Delete any unnecessary words.

Sentence 15: Correct the error in verb tense.

Index

a

Adjectives, descriptive
  of human characteristics, 56–57
  of place, 41–42
  of shape, 23–24
Adverbial clauses of time, 68–69
Adverbs, placement of, 8–9
Analogies, 125–26
Appositives, 86–88
Articles, 5–7, 35–37

c

Capitals, 20–22
Categorizing data, 105–7
Clauses
  nonrestrictive relative, 54–55, 99–101
  subordinate, 142–43
Cleft sentences, 159–61
Cohesive devices
  demonstratives, 140–41
  noun replacements, 118–22
Colons to introduce categories, 99–101
Commas
  with adverbial clauses, 68–69
  with appositives, 86–87
  with conditional sentences, 174–76
  with nonrestrictive relative clauses, 54–55

Commas (*cont.*)
   with participial phrases, 69–70
   with a series of items, 20–22
   with subordinate clauses, 142–43
   with transitional phrases, 122–25, 178–81
Conciseness, 108–9
Conditional sentences, 174–76

d

Defining
   by classification, 97–116
   by comparison and contrast, 117–36
   by example, 83–96
Describing
   an event, 65–79
   an object, 17–31
   a personality, 51–64
   a place, 33–49
   a process, 3–16
Dividing a topic, 104–5

e

Expletive *there*, 156–59
Expressing hypothetical situations, 177–78
Expressing and supporting an opinion, 139–54
Expressing priorities, 162–65
Expressions of cause and effect, 178–81
Expressions of opinion, 144–47

i

Imperatives, 4–7
Indirect speech to support an opinion, 143–44

n

Nouns with expressions of quantity, 53–54

p

Parallel sentences, 126–27
Parallel structures
   with infinitives and gerunds, 88–90
   with *not only . . . but also*, 161–62

Participial phrases, 69–70
Passive voice, 84–85, 101–2
Periods, 20–22
Point of view, 72–73
Prepositions with expressions of place, 37–41
Pronoun reference, 52–53

q

Quotations
    punctuation, 143–44
    to support an opinion, 143–44

r

Ranking, 155–71
Relative clauses, nonrestrictive, 54–55
Relevancy of support, 57–59

s

Semicolons
    to join sentences, 126–27
    with transitional phrases, 122–25, 178–81
Sentence connectors
    of chronological order, 7–8
    of classification, 102–4
    of comparison and contrast, 122–25
    of exemplification, 88–90
Speculating, 173–85
Statements of reason, 147
Subject–verb agreement
    with *to be*, 18–20, 34–35
    with verbs other than *to be*, 5–7, 34–35
Subordinate clauses, 142–43

v

Verbs, action, 70–71
Verb tense
    past, 52
    past perfect, 66–67
    past progressive, 66–67
    present, 5–7
    present perfect, 98–99